Sandpaper People

Mary Southerland

HARVEST HOUSE PUBLISHERS

EUGENE, OREGON

Cover by Left Coast Design, Portland, Oregon

Cover photo © John Foxx/Alamy Limited

SANDPAPER PEOPLE
Copyright © 2005 by Mary Southerland
Published by Harvest House Publishers
Eugene, Oregon 97402
www.harvesthousepublishers.com

Library of Congress Cataloging-in-Publication Data
Southerland, Mary.
  Sandpaper people/ Mary Southerland.
    p. cm.
  ISBN 978-0-7369-1614-1 (pbk.)

  1. Christian life. 2. Interpersonal relations—Biblical teaching. 3. Interpersonal relations—Religious aspects—Christianity. I. Title.
  BV4501.3.S66 2005
  248.4—dc22   2005001911

Printed in the United States of America

To the three people in my life
who know me best
but still love me most.
My husband, Dan, is my best friend and greatest cheerleader.
My son, Jered, is the son every mother dreams of having.
My daughter, Danna, is the sparkle in my life.
I love you completely and thank God for the unique and precious
relationships we share.
You are my greatest teachers and deepest loves.

Acknowledgments

Thanks to my husband—Dan. *Sandpaper People* would not have been written without your love and support. Your faithful encouragement and unwavering faith in this project kept my hands on the keyboard and my heart seeking God's truth about difficult relationships. You continue to be the love of my life and my greatest cheerleader.

Thanks to my children—Jered and Danna. You are my greatest teachers. Thank you for loving your "sandpaper mom."

Thanks to Harvest House for believing in me as a writer. You have become family and friends.

Thanks to Yvonne Anderson and Beverly Greer. You graciously offered quiet places where I could escape to write.

Thanks to Hyldia Williams for the great idea of creating "Sandpaper People" emery boards.

Thanks to God, the Author and Finisher of my faith. Your stubborn love for me when I was unlovable is the very heart of this book. You are the Friend of wounded hearts. It is through Your unconditional love and absolute acceptance that I not only can love and accept myself, but my sandpaper people as well. Thank you for the relationship truths in Your Word that have changed my life and allowed me to see these abrasive people through Your eyes. Please accept this book as an offering of praise for all You have done in my relationships. All praise, honor and glory belong to You.

CONTENTS

A Word from Mary.   7

The Biggest Problem in the World   9

1. Be Loving: Recognize Their Worth. 13

2. Be Humble: Choose Against Pride 25

3. Be Accepting: Love Them—Just As They Are 41

4. Be Encouraging: Become Their Cheerleader 59

5. Be Patient: Learn to Endure 79

6. Be Forgiving: Forgive and Forget 93

7. Be Caring: Meet a Need. 109

8. Be Peaceful: Wage Peace. 127

9. Be Confrontational: Care Enough to Confront. 145

10. Be Strong: Develop Endurance 163

11. Be Thankful: Thank God for Them 177

12. Be Committed: Refuse to Walk Away 189

Study and Application Guide 195

Personal Journal. 243

Notes 255

A Word
from Mary

SANDPAPER PEOPLE ARE A REALITY of life. In my life, God has used difficult relationships as catalysts through which He has lovingly upset my comfortable plans and purposefully redirected what I thought were my safe and sound steps. The results have often been chaotic and unsettling—but have always been life-changing. A changed life is the bottom line for God, and the very reason He sent His Son to earth.

The learned truths and personal insights I share in this book are from my life, which has been forever altered through dealing with sandpaper people and learning to get along with people who rub me the wrong way. Difficult relationships have been the source of great pain as well as an invaluable conduit for God's utmost healing for me. I thank Him for each sandpaper person and for the opportunity to share this part of my journey with you. I pray that within these pages you will find new strength and fresh certainties that will prepare your heart and life to experience anew His unconditional love, His unrivaled grace, and His timeless truths through the unlikely servants we call sandpaper people.

ABOUT THE CHAPTERS. Each chapter of *Sandpaper People* is constructed to present God's truth in a simple and applicable format. Men and women from the Bible walk through each chapter, interacting with their own sandpaper people, working through difficult relationships in the same way you and I must deal with them today. I encourage you to approach each chapter with the objective of finding one new truth God has waiting for you, a truth you can plug into your daily walk and use to nourish your relationships.

ABOUT THE "SANDPAPER FACTS." As I began the research for this book, I kept tripping over interesting and unusual facts about sandpaper. I found myself amazed and amused by the way God has laced sandpaper throughout creation. It's everywhere! The "Sandpaper Facts" are simply a testimony of God's attention to detail, a fact I find extremely comforting in dealing with sandpaper people.

ABOUT THE BIBLE STUDIES. God's Word meets every need. Yet we often rely upon our limited strength and human tactics when dealing with sandpaper people instead of employing the infinite power of His Word. Each chapter will lead you through a step-by-step plan for learning, processing, and applying God's truth to every difficult relationship in your life. I pray the Word will become real in your life as you move through this book.

ABOUT YOUR PERSONAL JOURNAL. Several years ago, I found myself at the bottom of a pit called "clinical depression." There, I learned the intrinsic value and healing power of journaling. Recording painfully honest thoughts, fresh insights, new truths, and learned lessons is imperative to solid spiritual growth. I encourage you to use the journal as the record of the spiritual lamps that illuminate your path as God equips you to deal with sandpaper people.

The Biggest Problem in the World

WE LIVE IN A PROBLEM-FILLED WORLD. However, you will be thrilled to know I have discovered the biggest problem of all—people! In my opinion, if there were fewer people, there would be fewer problems. Every day, we face the daunting challenge of getting along with people. Some make it easy, and some don't. Some are kind and gentle, encouraging, and replenishing, while others drive us to the brink of insanity and beyond. It might shock and dishearten you to realize that the roughest sandpaper person in your life may very well be living right under your own roof. The only possibility more disturbing is that *we* are sandpaper people. Understanding that we can all be abrasive at one time or another is an important admission in the quest to effectively deal with difficult relationships. However, there are those people who live in abrasive mode, day in and day out.

One Sunday morning, a Sunday school teacher, in the process of teaching the Ten Commandments to her third-grade class, asked the question, "Last week we learned the commandment to honor your father and mother. Can anyone tell me if there is one that refers to brothers and sisters?" A little girl's hand immediately shot up. When the teacher called on her to give an answer, the anxious youngster quickly responded, "Yes, there *is* a command-ment just about brothers. The one that says, 'Thou shalt not kill!' "

Let's be honest—some people are simply more difficult to get along with than others. They "rub" us the wrong way. I call them "sandpaper people." Sandpaper people come in all shapes, sizes, and colors—and sometimes they are *us!* We try to change them, run from them, ignore them, and even take a stab at fixing them. If only it were that simple. It rarely is.

When it comes to these problematical relationships, I have good news and bad news. The bad news is that sandpaper people are forever with us. The good news is that God has a plan for us to help us get along with people who rub us the wrong way. By making the choice to love as He loves, we can turn these sand-paper people into velvet people and in the process learn how to love the unlovable, just as God loves us. (It is crucial to note that God's relationship principles are rooted in and flow from a per-sonal relationship with Him. When our relationship with Him is right, every other relationship in life has the potential to be right. The choice is ours to make.)

We are called to wage peace. Jesus beautifully illustrates this truth in His selection of the 12 disciples. What a bag of mixed nuts! I have often wondered why God chose these ordinary men to do such extraordinary work. I certainly would have made dif-ferent choices. Among the group were four fishermen, a tax col-lector, and a religious zealot—different men, chosen to minister to different people in many different ways—but all called to live in peace and unity by the One they followed. I am certain there were fervent differences of opinion and fiery personality clashes from time to time. Each man came with his own agenda and plan. After all, they didn't choose each other. That choice was made for them by God and according to His plan.

As in the life of Jesus, God often arranges our circumstances based on the principle of opposites, so to speak. For example, if we need more patience, He surrounds us with irritating people. If we need to be more loving, unlovable people will cross our path until we learn to share the unconditional love we have found in God. If we need to learn self-control, emotional button-pushers will descend in droves, providing ample opportunity for us to practice anger-management skills. Just as the disciples were called to harmony and peace, so are we. Our relationships should not only demonstrate the reality of a living God, but total acceptance and wholehearted commitment as well. For the sandpaper people in your life, you may be God with "skin on"—the very definition of love and validation for them. Jesus tells us that "love for one another will prove to the world that you are my disciples" (John 13:35 NLT). A disciple is a follower, an imitator of the one he follows. Disciples study their master, longing to be just like him, deliberately choosing to do what he does, go where he goes, and say what he says. With every breath, every choice, and every step, a disciple grows more like his master. How can we deal with sandpaper people in a way that honors God? The answer is actually quite simple: by discovering and applying God's relationship principles as we choose daily to become a fully devoted follower of Jesus Christ, living as He lived and loving as He loved.

SANDPAPER BEGINNINGS

Sandpaper was first used in thirteenth-century China. A crushed-seashell mixture was stuck to parchment using natural gum adhesives. The idea resurfaced in Switzerland about 200 years ago. Crushed glass was glued to paper. Broken glass was neither sharp enough nor hard enough, so the search began for a material with the hardness of diamonds.

In the late 1800s, a method was perfected whereby sand and sawdust were heated to produce silicon carbide. A simulated sapphire, about one-fortieth the hardness of diamonds, can be made from aluminum oxide, the hardest commonly available abrasive. The degree of hardness is reflected in the price.

Sandpapers conform to the same numerical system. No. 60 means there are 60 grit particles to an inch; the smaller the number, the coarser the paper. Sandpaper is a precise material. All particles in a single grade must be exactly the same size. Even one oversize particle would cause a scratch.[1]

one

Be Loving:
Recognize Their Worth

We are God's workmanship.

Ephesians 2:10

T HE ARTIST CAME TO THE PARK every day at the same time, when the light was just right, positioning his easel and paints under the same familiar shade tree. It was his favorite spot to work and the perfect setting in which to satisfy his passion for painting. A talented and sensitive man, he specialized in portraits, skillfully drawing out the inner qualities of his subject. For hours, he watched the people strolling by, searching for just the right face to paint. He loved the way each face told many different stories, some filled with joy and others with pain and sadness, but all filled with life.

A homeless man sitting across the path caught the artist's eye. Thinking of God's handiwork in every human being, he resolved to paint the man as he imagined he could be. With the last stroke, he breathed a sigh of satisfaction, a contented smile spreading across his face. It was done. And it was some of his best work. The artist then called the man over to see the painting. "Is that me?" he asked. "That is the 'you' I see!" replied the artist. The man stared at the painting silently. Finally, with tears in his eyes, he softly declared, "If that's the man you see in me, then that's the man I'm going to be!"

SANDPAPER PEOPLE DESPERATELY NEED someone who will look beyond their abrasive behavior and rough exterior to recognize their worth. Somewhere along the way, sandpaper people have allowed someone or something to assign an identity to them that is false. Parents, friends, family members, or even enemies have shaped a distorted identity, producing a sandpaper person. As a result, sandpaper people live a life they were never intended to live, bound to an unhealthy self-image and having no concept of who they really are or what they can possibly become. Desperate to fit in, they try on different identities like new clothes and wonder why none of them fit. Sandpaper people have either not heard or refuse to believe the good news that their identity was established before the world began—in the heart and mind of God.

The words of Psalm 139 beautifully express the heart of God toward each and every one of us.

> You created my inmost being;
>   you knit me together in my mother's womb.
> I praise you because I am fearfully and wonderfully made;
>   your works are wonderful,
>   I know that full well.
>
> My frame was not hidden from you
>   when I was made in the secret place.
> When I was woven together in the depths of the earth,
>   your eyes saw my unformed body.
> All the days ordained for me
>   were written in your book
>   before one of them came to be (verses 13-16).

A healthy self-image is not one of pride or arrogance, but one that coincides with God's viewpoint. It is choosing to accept God's evaluation, learning to see ourselves as God sees us, agreeing with who we are in His eyes, and giving Him permission to make us what He designed us to be. In His eyes, every person is valuable—sandpaper and all. Sinful and broken, wounded and sick, sandpaper people are why He came. With tenacity and stubborn love, He pursues those whom others only shun—like the woman at the well.

> Eventually he came to the Samaritan village of Sychar, near the parcel of ground that Jacob gave to his son Joseph. Jacob's well was there; and Jesus, tired from the long walk, sat wearily beside the well about noontime. Soon a Samaritan woman came to draw water, and Jesus said to her, "Please give me a drink." He was alone at the time because his disciples had gone into the village to buy some food. The woman was surprised, for Jews refuse to have anything to do with Samaritans (John 4:5-9 NLT).

The woman at the well is the perfect example of a sandpaper person who was transformed by the One who looked beyond her flawed humanity to recognize the worth of her soul. In dealing with the difficult people in our lives, we must do what Jesus did in the life of this woman.

1. JESUS LOVED HER

Little is known about this woman, and what we do know isn't good. She was immoral and spiritually ignorant, an outcast despised by the Jews and even by her own people. She was very popular with the men of the village, who used her to satisfy their own physical desires and then tossed her aside like a broken, damaged, and used doll. I am certain this woman had no illusions and knew she meant nothing to these men. In the beginning she may have convinced herself they cared for her and perhaps even loved her, but I imagine that notion was short-lived. In fact, while studying her life, I have many times wondered if there had ever been a man in her life she could love or trust.

I don't know what drove the woman at the well to pursue such an empty and futile existence, but I do know, as far as Jesus was concerned, her old life was over! It didn't matter to Him. He looked at this woman through eyes of healing and forgiveness and saw His precious child. He just loved her—right where she was and just as she was. It's very clear in the scriptural account that this woman at the well was extremely important to Jesus. He recognized her worth.

Getting along with people who rub us the wrong way requires a new point of view, choosing to see them as God sees them, laying aside every attitude that does not reflect the image and heart of God. Sandpaper people are created in His image, and should be treated that way.

2. JESUS PURSUED HER

The woman at the well was so important to Jesus that He pursued her, going out of His way to arrange a meeting with her, a meeting she knew nothing about. Jesus was on His way to Galilee from Judea. In His day, the Jews hated the Samaritans and would never purposely travel through their land. There were other roads, better and safer roads, Jesus could have taken and usually did take—but not today. Today He had a divine appointment. Today He chose to go through the region of Samaria, through Sychar, the small village where this woman lived. Meeting this woman was no accident on the part of Jesus Christ. With great determination and forethought, He planned a divine interruption in her life, an interlude in which His love and forgiveness met her at the point of her greatest need. He planned to set her free!

The life of this woman reminds me of the little boy who built a wooden boat. For hours he worked, whittling and carving until it was exactly as he had dreamed it would be. After sanding and painting it he raced outside to the nearby river, where the launch of his cherished creation took place. Every day, the young captain sailed his boat up and down the quiet river, his active imagination weaving tales of pirates and treasures, mermaids and sea monsters—every story ending with the return of his seafaring ship.

hen our messes meet His mercy it is the perfect setting for a miracle!

Then one day, after a torrential rain, the little boy sailed his prized boat on the near-flood-stage stream. Too late, he realized the swift current was taking his boat out of reach. He frantically tried to retrieve it, but it was moving too fast and he soon ran out of shoreline to chase after it. The boat was lost. Heartbroken, he stood on the bank of the river, staring as his precious boat sailed away from him.

Several days later, he was returning home from school when he passed the toy store. The display window stopped him in his tracks. Rubbing his eyes, the youngster thought he must be dreaming because there, in the window, was his boat! Someone had found it! Dropping his backpack, he burst through the door and, with breathless wonder, told the owner that the boat in the window belonged to him. But the owner was not convinced and told the young man he would have to pay for the boat. "Can you please, please hold it for me?" he begged. "Just until the store closes today," the owner replied.

Frantic, but determined to have his boat, the little boy ran home, grabbed his piggy bank, and bolted back to the store and the waiting owner. Minutes later, he walked out of the toy store, leaving a broken and empty piggy bank behind, the boat securely in his hands. "You are twice mine, little boat," the boy whispered, "once because I made you, and once because I bought you."

Just as Jesus came looking for the Samaritan woman, He comes looking for you and for every abrasive or irritating sandpaper person as well, willing to step right into the sinful mess of our lives with the gift of healing love and restoration in His hands. When our messes meet His mercy it is the perfect setting for a miracle—and what a miracle it was! The price Jesus paid on the cross was enormous; but He gladly paid that price to buy back what He had created. Like this woman at the well, we are important because God made us and because He pursues us. This is the hope we find in Paul's words in the book of Romans: "God showed his great love for us by sending Christ to die for us while we were still sinners" (5:8 NLT)

3. JESUS VALUED HER

Sandpaper people simply cannot understand they are valuable to anyone, much less to God. Notice this woman's name is not even given in Scripture. Jesus simply called her "woman." I believe He was speaking not just to her, but to all women and to every need of a woman's life.

The fact that He spoke to her at all is a very strong declaration of her worth. In that day, women were considered inferior to men. A man didn't speak to a woman in public—even to his wife, mother, or sister. The role of the woman was restricted primarily to the home and family. But in the eyes of Jesus, this woman was someone of great value. I love the promise of Jeremiah 1:5: "Before I made you in your mother's womb, I chose you. Before you were born, I set you apart for a special work" (NCV). Our value rests solely in the eternal and undeniable fact we are created by God—set apart, planned, and wanted by Him! Sandpaper people will never be free to change until they understand that their worth and value comes from and flows through their identity in God.

4. JESUS CHOSE HER

Jesus not only loved and pursued the woman at the well, He also chose her! He chose this woman to carry out His plan. He wanted to reach the people of Samaria—the outcasts, the despised and rejected ones who would never be chosen by anyone for anything—in other words, the sandpaper people of Samaria.

I am certain Jesus could have made many other choices that would have made more sense and been more acceptable to His critics and His disciples. I can almost guarantee there were people in the village who were more moral than the woman at the well, and certainly women of greater integrity. Perhaps it would have been more fitting to select one of the leading women in the village to carry out the work of God. The choice of Jesus makes little sense to the human heart and reason—unless you factor in grace.

The grace of God changes everything! Grace can be simply defined as "God's riches at Christ's expense." God has always worked His greatest miracles through the most unlikely people and in the most improbable circumstances. What He chooses, He also cleanses. What He cleanses, He then molds. What He molds, He fills with His power—and what He fills, He always uses. We are His work of art.

Paul tells us in Ephesians 2:10 that we are "God's masterpiece. He has created us anew in Christ Jesus, so that we can do the good things he planned for us long ago" (NLT). Our value rests in the certain truth that we are chosen by God. We were chosen to do "good things" planned for us to do since before time began. We are neither an afterthought nor a mistake. There are no accidents with God. You and I were created in direct response to His love; our life plan was born out of His perfect plan.

Knowing that we are precious in His sight, that He pursues us tenaciously and passionately likes us, completely changes the entire foundation on which we live. When we grab hold of this momentous truth, hold it up against the backdrop of eternity, and begin to walk in the knowledge that we are worthy in His eyes—we will be set free! While sandpaper people long for that same freedom, they are imprisoned by the lie that they are unworthy of love from God or anyone else. Your sandpaper person needs to know he or she is chosen by God.

5. JESUS CHANGED HER

Most of us are determined to change every single sandpaper person we know. The result will ultimately be frustration and failure because the only one who can change a life is God. We live near the mountains of North Carolina, where woodworking is a common hobby and a unique art. When time permits, I love to browse through the old country stores—stores filled with quaint and unusual treasures and managed by some of the most interesting people I have ever met.

Several years ago, our family was on vacation and I was in search of a treasure. I decided it was time for an adventure so, taking an unmarked dirt road, I swerved and crept my way up the mountain until, rounding a hairpin turn, I spotted an old log cabin tucked way back in a clump of pine trees. A bearded man sat on the porch, rocking and whittling, a pile of wooden logs by his side. There on the rickety porch railing was a large collection of beautifully carved wooden dogs.

With a wave of his hand, the mountain man motioned for me to join him, the only invitation I needed. I parked the car, grabbed my purse, and made a beeline for those wooden dogs. "Look all ya want," the man invited me. "And if you need to, you can ask a question." I only had one. "How in the world do you carve these beautiful dogs out of those ordinary pieces of wood?" I asked. "Well, missy, it's pretty simple," he answered. "I just take me a piece of wood and cut away everything that don't look like a dog." That is exactly how God changes lives. He slowly, patiently uses the circumstances and relationships of life to cut away everything that doesn't look like His child. Some of us need extra work, but we can rest in the truth that if He is the One doing the cutting, the results will be astonishing.

The woman at the well was in desperate need of someone who could change her life. She asked Jesus,

> "You are a Jew, and I am a Samaritan woman. Why are you asking me for a drink?" Jesus replied, "If you only

knew the gift God has for you and who I am, you
would ask me, and I would give you living water." "But
sir, you don't have a rope or a bucket," she said, "and
this is a very deep well. Where would you get this
living water?"…Jesus replied, "People soon become
thirsty again after drinking this water. But the water I
give them takes away thirst altogether. It becomes a
perpetual spring within them, giving them eternal
life."

Longing and hope leaped into the woman's heart. "Please, sir, give
me some of that water! Then I'll never be thirsty again, and I
won't have to come here to haul water" (John 4:9-11,13-15 NLT).

The living water Jesus described is God's unconditional love,
a love that was completely foreign to the Samaritan woman. She
had spent her whole life going from man to man, desperately
searching for someone who would really love her. Notice she came
to the well at noontime, the hottest hour of the day, to draw her
water. Every other woman came in the morning or evening in
order to avoid the brutal heat. She came alone, I believe, to avoid
their condemning eyes and sarcastic whispers. I can only imagine
the loneliness she must have been feeling that day as she made her
way to the well.

Then she spotted Jesus—sitting at the well, waiting. The
minute she saw Him, she knew He had come for her, His eyes
filled with something she didn't quite understand. It was unconditional love that reached through her sin, drawing her to Him,
tearing down the guilt and stripping away the shame that had
become such a familiar part of her being. It was the unfailing love
for which we all thirst that compelled her to come. Real love,
God's love, with no conditions, no hidden clauses, and no strings
attached. Scripture tells us God is not just loving or able to dis-
pense love, but is the very definition and substance of love itself.
When we know Him, we know love. "Anyone who does not love
does not know God—for God is love. God showed how much he
loved us by sending his only Son into the world so that we might

have eternal life through him. This is real love. It is not that we loved God, but that he loved us and sent his Son as a sacrifice to take away our sins" (1 John 4:8-10 NLT).

Like this woman, we cannot give what we do not have. We are unable to give real love until we have received real love. It is only in a personal encounter with God that we can experience a love so powerful it reveals the very person of God to us. We must understand and remember that God does not love us because we are lovable and deserve to be loved. He loves us simply because He is love—and He cannot help Himself!

> We call it mercy—it is God's forgiving love.
> We call it fate—it is God's caring love.
> We call it kindness—it is God's accepting love.
> We call it death—it is God's proven love.
> We call it the plan of God—it is God's perfect love.
> We call it heaven—it is God's rewarding love.
> We call it eternity—it is God's unending love.

In the late 1800s, a group of women enrolled in a Bible study came across Malachi 3:3—"He will sit as a refiner and purifier of silver." Since no one understood the verse, they commissioned one of their number to explore the process of refining silver and report back to them at their next study. The woman called a silversmith, making an appointment to watch him work.

On the appointed day, she saw him hold a piece of silver over the fire, letting it heat up. He explained that in refining silver, one needed to hold the silver in the middle of the fire where the flames were hottest, so that all impurities would burn away. The woman thought about God holding us in such a hot spot; then she thought again about the verse, that he sits as a refiner and purifier of silver. She asked the silversmith if it was true he had to sit in front of the fire the whole time the silver was being refined. The man answered that he not only had to sit there holding the silver, but had to keep his eyes on the silver the entire time it was in the fire. If the silver was left even a moment too long in the flames, it would be destroyed. The woman was silent for a moment. Then she asked, "How do you know when the silver is fully refined?" He smiled. "Oh, that's easy. The refining process is complete when I see my image in it."

When we make the choice to love a sandpaper person, we are inviting God to work in us and through us to bring about change—to create His image in us so we can see His image in others. Difficult relationships and combative interactions do not hold up well in an atmosphere of love, because it is through love that stubborn wills are compelled to yield. Under the influence of God's love in our lives, winning no longer seems important to us, and we recognize the value and worth of a soul.

SANDPAPER BEAUTY

Beauty tip #1: An emery board is simply sandpaper on a stick, great to use on fingernails, toenails, and heels. Simply rub an emery board across rough heels. Follow with olive oil or petroleum jelly.

Beauty tip #2: Keep your lips looking great throughout the year, even in winter months, by using sandpaper to remove the damaged skin.

Beauty tip #3: One of the most primitive methods of hair removal was used by women as late as the 1940s. It involved rubbing skin with mitts or discs that had the abrasiveness of fine sandpaper. Give it a try! Cut a strip of 400- to 600-grit sandpaper. Wrap it around a small wooden cube or rubber spatula and *gently,* working on one small area at a time, rub in small circles one way, then small circles the other—until the hair is gone. Do not scrub or rub up and down. Gentleness is the key. Finish with body lotion to moisturize the area. Your skin will glow and feel great!

two

Be Humble:
Choose Against Pride

*God opposes the proud
but gives grace to the humble.*
James 4:6

Born and raised in Texas, I'm a proud native through and through. Texans are known for their boisterous state pride, and I am no exception. I especially enjoy the constant barrage of jokes because of my heritage, delighting in their humor—part truth and part lore—at the expense of myself and every other Texan. Here's a favorite!

Two Texans were trying to impress each other with the size of their ranches. One asked the other, "What's the name of yours?" The rancher replied, "The Rocking R, ABC, Bar U, Staple Four, Box D, Rolling M, Rainbow's End, Silver Spur Ranch." Duly impressed, the questioner exclaimed, "Wow—that's sure some name! How many head of cattle do you run?" With a sad shake of his head, the other answered, "Not many. Most don't survive the branding." And so it is with pride. Very few survive this deadly disease.

C.S. Lewis called pride a deadly disease, a "spiritual cancer" that devours love and contentment. Pride is a sign of our own insecurity and feelings of inferiority. In reality, pride and inferiority are opposite sides of the same coin, and both are sin, a preoccupation with self that leaves little room for God's spirit of humility. Spurgeon poetically warned us not to be proud of "race, face, or place."

We all struggle with pride and must constantly battle the tendency to measure every circumstance and relationship against the narcissistic "what's in it for me?" viewpoint. Pride has no place in the life of a Christian and will surely lead to unhealthy relationships and the inability to deal with those difficult people who rub us the wrong way. In an effort to strip away the power of God, pride steps between Him, us, and His provision for healthy relationships that honor Him. James says it well—"God opposes the proud but gives grace to the humble" (4:6). The fact that God stands in opposition against prideful people is a strong and sobering thought and should send us running to the place of humility.

Because He is a loving Father, God opposes pride, in part, for what it does to His children. "Pride will destroy a person; a proud attitude leads to ruin. It is better to be humble and be with those who suffer than to share stolen property with the proud" (Proverbs 16:18-19 NCV). Learning to deal with pride is an essential part of every relationship and when it comes to getting along with people who rub us the wrong way, an imperative choice we must make. Pride will prevent us from seeing that difficult person as God sees them. Pride will hold us back from laying down our expectations and rights in order to reach out to the sandpaper people who cross our path. Pride will slowly erode the humble spirit God so wants to see in His people and in their relationships.

I suspect that a good dose of humility would cure many of our ailing relationships with sandpaper people because humility always bows to the needs of others while crucifying our rights and demands. Then the question becomes, how can we rid our lives of pride and prevent it from carving out a destructive stronghold from which relationship problems arise? The answer is found in a passage of Scripture written by the apostle Paul and directed to the church in Rome.

> By the grace given me I say to every one of you: Do not think of yourself more highly than you ought, but rather think of yourself with sober judgment, in accordance with the measure of faith God has given you. Just as each of us has one body with many members, and these members do not all have the same function, so in Christ we who are many form one body, and each member belongs to all the others. We have different gifts, according to the grace given us...Be devoted to one another in brotherly love. Honor one another above yourselves (Romans 12:3-6,10).

Paul certainly understood what it meant to struggle with pride. Before his encounter with Christ, he had been a man of great arrogance, a power broker in the government as well as a highly regarded persecutor of anyone following Jesus. Little did Paul know what the road to Damascus held for him that day when God interrupted his life with His blinding love and unparalleled power. Everything changed. Paul became a humble man, the walking definition of a servant, delighting in his new role of striving to be last among the least. It is from such a life of humility that the apostle offers five steps you and I can take in order to prevent pride and effectively interact with sandpaper people.

STEP 1: RECOGNIZE THE POWER OF GRACE

> By the grace given me I say to every one of you...
> (Romans 12:3).

Paul was a trophy of grace, his heart captured by grace and his life completely transformed in the process. In everything he did, through every act of service he gave or received, with every breath he took and every word he spoke, God's grace was triumphantly at work. God's grace was Paul's starting place, his finish line, and everything in between—the very reason he was so humble, his life so powerful.

It is such a paradox in God's design for life that in order to be strong we must choose weakness; in order to be first we must be content with last place; and in order to genuinely accept and love sandpaper people, we must relocate our position in life to the lowest place possible. Our offended heart cries out, though in sheer humanness, for justice to be applied in the life of that difficult person.

However, sandpaper people long for and even demand mercy, desperately hoping they won't get what they deserve. But all of us—any of us—would give anything we have and everything we are in order to receive *grace*. The amazing truth is that grace is ours for the asking. God stands ready to pour His priceless grace into every heart and soul; grace works to generate unexplainable peace, eternal life, unending joy, and freedom from sin through unconditional love. Grace offers us the riches of God at the expense of Jesus Christ and His death on the cross.

Pride's goal is to make us independent of God, duping us into believing we are in control of our own fate and are able to call our own shots. What audacity we possess as humans, to think we can live life on our own when, whether we admit it or not, we are totally dependent upon God, and even our very next breath is a gift from His hand. Pride convinces us we can play God, worshiping ourselves while erecting false idols upon rebellion and sin. Pride is the universal religion of hell and a deadly poison in every difficult relationship. As long as we come in pride, unbroken and unyielding, we will never find victory in dealing with sandpaper people. But when we clothe our hearts in humility, choosing against pride and selfish desires, even the most difficult people we encounter will soften under the loving grip of grace.

A friend recently told me about a new product she found listed on the Internet. "Disposable Guilt Bags" first appeared in a few select stores to test the market. You could buy a set of these bags—

ten ordinary brown bags on which were printed the following instructions: "Place the bag securely over your mouth, then take a deep breath and blow out all of your guilt. Close the bag and dispose of immediately." The amazing part of this story is, the Associated Press reported more than 2500 kits had sold immediately at $2.50 per kit. Unbelievable! (Actually, it isn't. Guilt is the gift that keeps on giving. We'll do almost anything to escape it.)

Sandpaper people know much about guilt and little about grace. Nevertheless, grace is what they seek. I know how hard it is to respond with grace when the actions of a sandpaper person push you over the edge, but that is exactly the place where grace should thrive and shine best.

When Frederick II, an eighteenth-century king of Prussia, went on an inspection tour of a Berlin prison, he was greeted with the cries of prisoners hoping and praying for leniency. They fell on their knees, pleading their cases, asserting their innocence, and declaring their unjust imprisonment. While listening to these mournful prostestations of innocence, Frederick's eye was caught by a solitary figure in the corner, a prisoner sitting quietly and all alone. "Why are you here?" Frederick asked him. "I am here for armed robbery, Your Majesty." "Are you guilty?" the king asked. "Oh yes, Your Majesty. I entirely deserve my punishment," the prisoner replied. Frederick called the jailer. "Release this guilty man at once," he instructed. "I will not have him kept in this prison, where he will undoubtedly corrupt all of these innocent people."

Nothing on this earth is powerful enough to erase guilt—we must deal with it. We try to "fix" ourselves but fail. We try to "fix" sandpaper people but fail. The only power that can make forgiveness a reality is God's grace. "In Christ we are set free by the blood of his death. And so we have forgiveness of sins because of God's rich grace" (Ephesians 1:7 NCV). When our lives are lived against the backdrop of grace, pride will die from a lack of attention.

STEP 2: TAKE CHARGE OF YOUR MIND

Do not think of yourself more highly than you ought,
but rather think of yourself with sober judgment, in
accordance with the measure of faith God has given
you (Romans 12:3).

Pride loves to take up residence in an undisciplined thought
life, changing the focus and dictating attitudes with little or no
resistance. When Paul encouraged the believers in Rome to cultivate "sober judgment," he was warning them to take charge of the
mind, refusing to allow the entrance of any thoughts that would
entertain pride. When it comes to dealing with those who rub us
the wrong way, a disciplined thought life is vital to surviving that
relationship, and certainly to thriving in it.

I have heard it said that the bigger a man's head gets, the easier
it is to fill his shoes. It is not wrong for Christians to recognize and
even applaud gifts in their own lives and in the lives of others, as
long as we remember that spiritual gifts are ours to manage, not
to own. Pride draws attention to those God-given gifts and tempts
us to take credit for their existence and the way in which they are
used.

Sandpaper people tend to find worth and identity in what
they do—not who they are. As a result, their actions are planned
with the thought of drawing the attention of anyone and everyone
in a vain effort to establish self-worth. To the sandpaper person,
all attention is good, and they will gain it in any way possible. Our
responsibility is to love and accept these difficult people without
insisting they change or counting on them to change. In order to
do that, we must choose grace and humility—not pride and censure. Pride vanishes beneath the loving gaze of our Father, who
simply longs for each one of us to see ourselves through His eyes.

A famous explorer in South America was once forced to
abandon his journey by an almost invisible enemy. The voyager
was equipped to meet leopards, serpents, and crocodiles. They
proved to be no threat, but what he had failed to consider were the

tiny insects called chiggers, a kind of tropical flea. Someone com-
posed this poem about these tiny invaders:

> Here's to the chigger, the bug that's no bigger
> Than the end of a very small pin;
> But the itch that he raises simply amazes,
> And that's where the rub comes in!

Pride and chiggers have a lot in common. Pride attacks in little
ways, by unseen actions and subtle thoughts. Unguarded attitudes
and random thoughts are prime breeding grounds for pride. We
must take charge of those thoughts and discipline our attitudes
while training our thinking processes to give up and obey God.

We are in a war for the control of the mind. The thought life
is the frontline of battle for every believer. Paul recognizes that
truth, and in 2 Corinthians 10:5, urges us on in the battle: "We are
taking every thought captive to the obedience of Christ" (NASB).
To take something captive is a military tactic we would do well to
employ because the harsh reality is that, when it comes to our
thought life, we are in a mighty war—especially when dealing
with sandpaper people. Sometimes it seems as if these abrasive
persons can actually crawl into our minds, grab hold of any undisciplined thoughts floating around, and fling them into our hearts
as attitudes laced with burning arrogance and prideful percep-
tions of who we are in comparison. But we can change our lives
by changing the way we think. We can dictate our heart attitudes
by fixing our thoughts on God and His truth. The result is peace,
which stands against pride, electing humility instead. "You will
keep in perfect peace all who trust in you, whose thoughts are
fixed on you" (Isaiah 26:3 NLT).

What does it mean to "fix" our thoughts? Webster's Dictionary
defines "fixed" as "rigid, solid, or firm." We must learn to establish
our thoughts solidly on the truth of God's Word. We need to be
rigid in controlling our thinking processes, holding firm to God's
standard for the mind. The result will be a stable way of thinking

and a disciplined pattern of living. To prevent pride requires a choice to take charge of our mind.

STEP 3: BE A KINGDOM THINKER

> Just as each of us has one body with many members, and these members do not all have the same function, so in Christ we who are many form one body (Romans 12:4-5).

In order to prevent pride we must be kingdom people, people who see the big picture. Sandpaper people have tunnel vision and are usually concerned only with what affects them. In dealing with them, it is easy for us to inadvertently slide into their way of thinking. But in doing so, we lose sight of God's kingdom plan and purpose. Every believer has a gift that is meant to help the body of Christ grow and achieve balance.

When we were living in Fort Lauderdale, our neighbors had a pool we all enjoyed on those brutally hot and humid summer days. At first, I lamented the fact we couldn't afford to have a pool, but after watching my neighbor deal with the maintenance of his, I decided I had the best of both worlds.

> Sandpaper people need to know that the ground at the foot of the cross is level and that *whose* they are matters more than *who* they are.

Every time I turned around, he was either going to or returning from the pool-supply store. It seemed that keeping the level of chemicals in balance was an almost impossible task. My neighbor fought the battle well, but still, the recurrent algae taxed his patience and his checkbook. Finally, after several bouts with the green slime, my weary neighbor surrendered, hiring a professional pool service to do the job. Success resulted, and the pool stayed beautiful and algae-free because of the right chemical balance.

Balance is hard to maintain—in swimming pools and in relationships—especially those relationships with sandpaper people. For the church and the relationships within it to be balanced, every believer must function according to his or her God-given gifts. That is the plan. "A spiritual gift is given to each of us as a means of helping the entire church" (1 Corinthians 12:7 NLT). Spiritual gifts are neither toys nor weapons but rather tools God has placed in our hands to use in building His kingdom. When we focus on the gift instead of the Giver, we are missing the big picture, the kingdom picture, and we'll find it easy to become a prisoner of pride, thinking that we have arrived and are more spiritual than others. Pride destroys unity and sets itself up against God, a very dangerous place to be. Every gift, every believer, and every relationship is important and has a unique purpose in the kingdom. God is all about relationships. The very fact that He moved heaven and earth in order to make a relationship possible between Him and us is nothing short of miraculous.

We may believe our sandpaper person has little or nothing to offer in the way of serving God, but Scripture is clear that, if they are believers, they are part of the plan and are gifted to serve. Is Romans 8:28 true when it says that "all" things work together for our good? To propose any other interpretation is to negate the Word of God. It is true that God uses all life offers, the good and bad circumstances as well as the difficult and easy relationships, to work good in our lives and in His kingdom. Sandpaper people need to know that the ground at the foot of the cross is level and that *whose* they are matters more than *who* they are. Our own pride keeps us from seeing those abrasive people as God sees them and loving them as God loves them. We need to choose His perspective on difficult people, knowing that His grace covers them just as it covers us.

STEP 4: PRACTICE ACCOUNTABILITY

Each member belongs to all the others (Romans 12:5).

Accountability is often seen as a relationship straitjacket, which limits freedom of expression and hinders those who "march to the beat of a different drummer." Actually, the opposite is true. Accountability frees us to grow and change and is an important part of every relationship. Furthermore, when it comes to getting along with people who rub us the wrong way, accountability is mandatory. Accountability must be mutual in order to be healthy and effectual. When we willingly make ourselves accountable to others, we are creating a hedge of protection that ultimately forms boundaries, parameters, and behavioral lines that should not be crossed in any relationship.

Sandpaper people have experienced very little accountability in life because at the core of being accountable to someone is the willingness to be submissive to them. The difficult relationships in life are not usually ones in which submission has been considered important, let alone necessary, because neither person involved is willing to submit to the other. I believe that in many relationships, sandpaper or otherwise, a choice to submit would translate the language of the entire relationship into a completely new one—that of love.

Accountability is often avoided because we have abused the concept of submission. God never intended submission to be anything other than a *gift* to every relationship. Submission is not meant to be demeaning and does not involve slavery in any form, physical or emotional. Submission is protection and an intentional willingness to consider the desires and wishes of another before our own. God places people in our lives to see things we cannot see, to encourage and build us up, to correct, love, and protect us.

Our son, Jered, has always had an innate ability to picture the way things should be, not as they are. I first realized the strength of his gift when he was ten years old. Summers in South Florida always brought an afternoon shower or thunderstorm. A sheet of water would pour from one particular spot in the gutter, and it bore a strong resemblance to Niagara Falls, which meant we would be drenched if we dared to open the front door and venture outside. We obviously had a drainage problem!

After being soaked one too many times, Dan, my husband, marched out to the garage, grabbed his ladder and tool box and, with an air of determination, set out on his mission to find the drainage problem and eliminate it! An hour went by with no solution in sight. When the second hour produced only frustration and loud banging noises, Jered mercifully decided to save his dad and us from a likely drowning. He stepped outside, closed the door behind him, and commenced his inspection of the gutter dilemma. After several minutes had passed, he offered his expert opinion. "Dad, if you move that piece to the left and connect it to that other piece, I think it might take care of the problem." Dan did as he was directed. When both father and son stepped back to survey their work, a now smiling and triumphant Dan turned to his obviously brilliant son and said, "Where were you two hours ago?" The summer storms came, but the front-porch floods vanished. Since that day, when Dan has a repair problem, the first person he calls is Jered. My husband is a very wise man in many ways, but one of the most important lessons I have learned from him is to surround myself with people who will hold me accountable and share new perspectives.

We tend to view accountability as a crutch and submission as a weakness when, in reality, submission is harnessed strength—a controlled strength born out of obedience to God. The apostle Paul gives us the basis for submission in Ephesians 5:21: "Submit to one another out of reverence for Christ." The word "reverence" can also be translated as "worship." And there we have the true reason for submitting to God and to others. Submission is worship. To worship God in our relationships ensures His presence and power at work in those relationships. God inhabits worship.

In the deserts of Arabia lived an expert guide called "Dove Man," known for his tracking skills and the fact that he never lost his way. The secret of his success was that he carried with him a homing pigeon that had a very fine cord attached to one of its legs. When he had doubts as to which path to take, he threw the bird into the air. The pigeon pulled the cord in the direction of home, accurately leading the guide to his goal. We always need connections to those who will point us in the right direction. We will take the wrong path or make a wrong turn and...there will be times when we have no idea which way to go or how to get home. We must then turn to God and to those who hold us accountable.

Jesus submitted Himself to the will of His father. He willingly laid down his desires and dreams, His plans and hopes, in total submission to God in order to save a world filled with sandpaper people. And out of that total surrender came the most powerful life ever lived. When we are willing to submit ourselves to God and make ourselves accountable to others, we are making choices that will prevent pride and make difficult relationships easier to navigate.

STEP 5: SERVE OTHERS

Be devoted to one another in brotherly love. Honor one another above yourselves (Romans 12:20).

Because I am basically a self-centered person, the last thing I usually want to do is to serve someone who is hard to get along with and rubs me the wrong way. In fact, the way I figure it, *they* should be serving *me* in order to make up for all of the grief they have caused. Sandpaper people are hard to serve and hard to help because they rarely, if ever, think of themselves as someone in need. The needs of others are not high on their priority list, but control and power definitely are. To manipulate is to succeed. Sandpaper people honestly believe the world does or should revolve around them. It doesn't seem to matter if the audience is applauding or jeering. Either way, they win.

When we dare to serve a sandpaper person, it rocks their world. They are so accustomed to scratching and clawing their way to a false and shallow acceptance that they find it almost impossible to believe anyone would ever be willing to serve them in any way—without ulterior motives, that is. That kind of chosen love is foreign to them, but it certainly grabs their attention. It is after we have loved and served the sandpaper people in our lives that we begin to see them with different eyes.

Scripture tells us we must honor and be devoted to one another. "Devotion" indicates commitment and duty and carries the idea of a constant faithfulness that deliberately chooses to serve repeatedly. To "honor" someone means to "prefer" him or her or regard them as more important than ourselves. Most sandpaper people are accustomed to people preferring that they disappear. I am convinced, if we learn to look past the irritating antics of sandpaper people and simply love them and "prefer" them, a transformation will begin not only in their lives but in our relationship with them as well. In the book of Philippians, Paul explains that when we are serving others we are doing what Jesus did:

> Is there any encouragement from belonging to Christ? Any comfort from his love? Any fellowship together in the Spirit? Are your hearts tender and sympathetic? Then make me truly happy by agreeing wholeheartedly with each other, loving one another, and working together with one heart and purpose. Don't be selfish; don't live to make a good impression on others. Be humble, thinking of others as better than yourself. Don't think only about your own affairs, but be interested in others, too, and what they are doing. Your attitude should be the same that Christ Jesus had (Philippians 2:1-5 NLT).

These words of Paul are telling us that when we choose to love and serve others, especially those who are difficult to love, we have the same attitude Jesus had. Someone once told me, "He that falls in love with himself will have no rivals." My mother generally summarized her feelings about anyone who was arrogant or prideful by announcing, "If I could buy him for what he's *really* worth, and sell him for what he *thinks* he's worth I'd be a millionaire!"

I once heard a missionary who was trying to do translation work in a particular tribe tell how difficult it was to translate the word *pride*, or at least the concept of one who is proud. Finally, he came up with the idea to use the tribe's native expression of "the ears being too far apart." The phrase conveyed the idea of having an "inflated head"—which is probably hard to improve on when we talk about the nature of pride.

When our head is filled with thoughts of self, when our hearts are determined to love ourselves before others, or when we serve only for the applause of men, we will become arrogant, and our service becomes an offense to God. Micah 6:8 outlines what God wants to see in the way we handle relationships: "The Lord has told you...what is good. He has told you what he wants from you: to do what is right to other people, love being kind to others, and live humbly, obeying your God" (NCV). Peter Marshall, the famous preacher, once prayed, "Lord, when we are wrong, make us willing to change, and when we are right, make us easy to live with." How true!

Corrie Ten Boom loved to tell the story about a proud woodpecker who was tapping away at a dead tree. When the sky unexpectedly turned black and the thunder began to roll, undaunted, the feathered carpenter went right on working. Suddenly a bolt of lightning struck the tree, splintering it into hundreds of pieces. Startled but unhurt, the haughty bird flew off, screeching to his feathered friends, "Hey, everyone, look what I did! Look what I did!"

That old woodpecker reminds me of people who think more highly of themselves than they should. Usually they are so busy bragging about their "achievements" and self-made greatness that they fail to recognize God as the source of all their abilities. In short, sandpaper people suffer from spiritual delusions of grandeur. Without the Lord, no one amounts to anything, and in our own strength, we cannot please Him. The words of 1 Peter 5:6 should be our watchword in life: "Humble yourselves under the mighty power of God, and in his good time he will honor you" (NLT).

⌒

Pride sets a relationship up for failure. Pride and arrogance fuel conflict and erect emotional walls. We must choose against pride and for humility in dealing with sandpaper people. In fact, I suspect that the refusal to purge prideful thoughts, attitudes, habits, and behavior is one of the main reasons difficult relationships exist. When we choose to be humble before God, submitting in love to sandpaper people, we are walking in an obedience that pleases God. And this obedience infuses into the most difficult relationships the possibility of transforming sandpaper people into velvet people.

SANDPAPER LEARNING

Sandpaper numbers (numbers cut from sheets of sandpaper) provide children with an opportunity to feel the number as they begin the visual process of recognizing the numeral and learn the physical process of writing it.

Sandpaper numbers stimulate a child's senses to maximize learning. The teacher sits on the child's dominant side when presenting a lesson. If the child is right-handed, the teacher sits to his or her right to ensure that perception of the lesson is optimized.

The teacher takes each number out of the box and traces it two or three times with their finger, then asks the child to trace the number. After the child is familiar with the number, the teacher repeats the process, saying the number aloud. [2]

three

Be Accepting:
Love Them—Just As They Are

Love one another as I have loved you.
John 15:12 NKJV

As the mother of two of them, I am convinced that every teenager, at one time or another, is a sandpaper person. Of course, every teenager can say the same about their mother, but that's another story. While everyone in the Southerland household is prone to drama, it is usually our daughter, Danna, who is the source of our finest productions. Danna is a musician and dramatist in giftedness and by personality. In middle school, she went through a time when she daily bemoaned the fact she was unloved by everyone on the face of the earth.

On one particularly rough day in her teen world, I corrected her for some minor rule infraction and was totally unprepared for her emotional eruption. With admirable flamboyance, she threw herself on the couch, wailing with great gusto, "Nobody loves me!

Everybody hates me!" Her brother, Jered, was sitting at the kitchen table doing homework and without even looking up said, "That is *not* true, Danna." I was so proud of him and of the fact he wanted to reassure his sister of his love. I was so wrong. When Danna looked up in surprise at her brother's response, Jered turned to her and said gently, "It really isn't true that everybody hates you. Some people don't even know you yet."

Where God's Love Comes In

Well, so much for brotherly love, but that is where God's love comes in. It may surprise you to know that He doesn't love us because we're lovable. God loves us because He *is* love. He calls us to celebrate the differences in each other instead of insisting that sandpaper people change to meet our requirements. There must be threads of elasticity running through the fiber of our relationships with sandpaper people. The truth is, those who deserve love the least, need love the most. Just as we cannot allow others to define us, so we must stop trying to control, change, and define others.

It is imperative that we understand we cannot base love for these difficult people on feelings but on God's love, which is released when we choose to love that sandpaper person *as is.* In reality, we can't change them anyway. God has to do the changing if it is to be a lasting change. Our responsibility is to love them with a love that never gives up—with God's love.

As a pastor's wife, I often have the opportunity to love people who rub me the wrong way. It seems that ministry is overflowing with sandpaper people. Dan, my husband, was the pastor of Flamingo Road Church in Fort Lauderdale, Florida, for 13 years. During those years, I was involved in many areas, but my first love was the women's ministry. On the third Thursday of each month, hundreds of women gathered for a community Bible study and a time of connecting with God and with other women. As the Bible-study teacher, I prayed fervently that God would make me sensitive to the needs of every woman who attended. Consequently, I taught series on life issues—relevant topics I hoped would draw in those women who would ordinarily never set foot in a church. It worked! Each month, the number of visitors grew. Bank executives, housewives, secretaries, doctors—you name it—walked through the doors of our church, many for the first time!

As the years went by, I began to notice a different type of woman in the audience. Actually, she was no different from the others; she just looked different. Tattoos, multiple and strangely located body piercings, unusual and sometimes radically bizarre clothes stood out from heavily made-up faces. However, one thing was the same. Their eyes were filled with the pain of a broken life, silently pleading, *Can someone please help me?*

I learned many important lessons while teaching that Bible study. One of the most important lessons was that helping and serving people is messy. Sherry was my first real mess. I will never forget the first time I saw her, standing at the back of the auditorium looking utterly lost and completely out of place. She had seen a newspaper ad describing the series I was teaching: "In His Eyes," a study designed to lead women to the place of seeing themselves as God sees them, through eyes of love and with a heart of forgiveness. Sherry obviously needed to know she was loved and cherished by the living God who gave Himself for her. Several layers of makeup, suggestive clothes, and the smell of alcohol told me she was running as fast as she could from her sin, desperately hoping to find someone who cared enough to save her from herself.

She waited patiently for me as I prayed with and for a long line of hurting women. When the last of them had left, I walked over to Sherry and sat down beside her. In her eyes, I saw raw pain and a wounded heart, the results of a shattered life. I also saw the fear that I would turn away. I was the first to speak. "I am so glad you came tonight. How can I help you?" A sob escaped as she dissolved into tears. I took her hand and waited. It was as if an internal dam had broken and the raging waters of sin and shame were finally released.

Sherry had been raised in a Christian family, but at the age of 13, she decided she was ready to live life on her own. As days and weeks passed, she found herself in places she never thought she would be—and at the ripe old age of 14, she became a prostitute to support her drug and alcohol addictions. Sleep was a luxury she could no longer afford, unless it paid well. Food was either provided as part of her services to men or fished out of garbage cans lining back alleys. Cardboard boxes and newspapers became her bedding as the bottom fell out of her world, dropping her into a dark, slimy pit. A drug overdose landed her in the county hospital, where doctors delivered the ultimatum that if she didn't change her life, she would lose it. And one morning, a hospital volunteer gave her the newspaper in which we had placed the ad for our Bible study. "Somehow I knew I was supposed to be here tonight. Can you help me?" Sherry pleaded. My heart soared with the thrill of leading a lost lamb to the Shepherd as we read Scripture, prayed, and found the answers she had come seeking. Finally, she prayed, pleading with God to "please, fix my screwed-up life." It was a precious moment of transformation. When she asked if I would teach her how to live this new life, I decided right then and there that God needed my help in saving Sherry.

During the following weeks and months, I spent many hours teaching her how to study the Bible, how to pray, how to deal with her sin, and how to withstand temptation. She became my personal project—and I was failing miserably. She was on and off various drugs, always promising that this time would be her last. I often smelled alcohol on her breath, and she seemed much more interested in spending time with me than with God.

After several frustrating months, I finally realized I had indeed become Sherry's savior. And let me tell you, I make a lousy savior. There is only one true Savior, and I am not Him. I picked up the phone and called her, inviting her to a special lunch the next day. When she arrived, we ate and discussed her future. I let her go that day, relinquishing her to God. The results were amazing. She began to depend on Him instead of me. Other women stepped into her life as friends and mentors. As I began to accept and love her just as she was, Sherry was set free to become who God had intended her to be all along.

Love with No "P.S."

We sometimes accept someone with a hidden agenda in mind. That is especially true with sandpaper people. We can't wait to get our hands on them in order to remodel their annoying behavior and "fix" them, parading them in front of all so they can see our incredible new creation. That attitude is simply pride-driven tolerance. Tolerance says, "I accept you for now, but if you don't change in time, my offer of acceptance will expire." Acceptance says, "I accept you for who you are. Period! No strings attached." When we accept the sandpaper people in our life, we are relinquishing them, handing them over to the One who can change and restore them. Christ is then free to work in their lives, and they are His responsibility, not ours. With Sherry, my love had failed but God's love didn't and never does! His love is the only love that embraces the broken lives of sandpaper people. It is an unfailing love that never gives up.

A college man once walked into a photo shop with a framed picture of his girlfriend. "I'd like this picture duplicated, please." When the shop owner removed the picture from its frame, he noticed an inscription on its back.

> My dearest Tom,
> I love you with all of my heart.
> I love you more and more each day.
> I will love you forever and ever.
> I am yours for all of eternity.

The note was signed "Diane," and it contained a P.S.:

> If we ever break up,
> I want this picture back!

Love that never gives up has no "P.S." in it. Worldly love collapses and disintegrates under the emotional fire of conflict, but true love never fails. Sandpaper people are well acquainted with the self-serving love that does not withstand the radical pain they so often inflict. What they need is a true love, a love that doesn't collapse under the weight of testing! Strong and unconditional, it will not crumble at the feet of a crisis. True love is God's love, a love we can neither understand nor explain in human terms. His love is powerfully illustrated in the life of the Old Testament prophet Hosea.

> The LORD said to me again, "Go, show your love to a woman loved by someone else, who has been unfaithful to you. In the same way the LORD loves the people of Israel, even though they worship other gods and love to eat the raisin cakes." So I bought her for six ounces of silver and ten bushels of barley. Then I told her, "You must wait for me for many days. You must not be a prostitute, and you must not have sexual relations with any other man. I will act the same way toward you." In the same way Israel will live many days without a king or leader, without sacrifices or holy stone pillars, and without the holy vest or an idol. After this, the people of Israel will return to the LORD their God and follow him and the king from David's family. In the last days they will turn in fear to the LORD, and he will bless them. (Hosea 3:1-5 NCV)

Hosea was married to Gomer, definitely the main sandpaper person in his life. They had three children, and seemed happy together until Gomer blew it by being unfaithful to Hosea. Leaving him, she became a prostitute, selfishly clinging to her depraved desires, betraying his love, and breaking the covenant of marriage. Hosea had every right to walk away from Gomer and his commitment to her! No one would have blamed him, and most would have cheered him. But love that never fails calls us up to higher choices—supernatural choices that demand supernatural action! The lives of Hosea and Gomer present five choices that unfailing love makes. They are the choices we must make in dealing with abrasive people, choices empowered by a love that never gives up.

CHOICE 1: CHOOSE FAITHFULNESS

> The LORD said to me again, "Go, show your love to a woman loved by someone else, who has been unfaithful to you" (Hosea 3:1 NCV).

> I will make you my wife forever, showing you righteousness and justice, unfailing love and compassion. I will be faithful to you and make you mine (2:19-20 NLT)

Today's world knows little about faithfulness and fails to value it. Hosea had a decision to make. I am sure everything within him told him to run. His heart was broken; his home was on the brink of total destruction; his anger at an all-time high. The pain had to be excruciating as only emotional betrayal can be. He was embarrassed and felt like a fool. Everyone knew exactly what Gomer was doing because she was blatant in her sin and had been violating her husband's trust for a long time. Hosea wasn't even sure he was the father of his second and third children, but he chose to stay with Gomer because he resolved to honor his commitment to his wife in marriage and to his God in obedience. Sometimes being faithful means sacrificing your own happiness for a time in order to redeem the relationship. Hosea did just that. God called him to faithfulness and asked him to focus on his wife's needs instead of his own. He obeyed.

Sandpaper people rarely encounter such love. It's just too easy to walk away from them, refusing to engage in such difficult relationships. Sometimes, however, we have no choice. Our sandpaper person often sits across the breakfast table from us, shares our bed each night, or gave birth to us. It is those intimate but tough relationships that tutor us in facing and living with difficult people.

The prevalent mentality today in relationships is that of our instant-gratification society. If it doesn't work out, walk away. If it's too hard, don't do it. Protect your rights at all costs. Love only when it produces personal benefits. A love that never gives up creates a faithful heart and is the only hope for dealing successfully with the sandpaper people in our lives.

CHOICE 2: CHOOSE TO FORGIVE

> The LORD said to me again, "Go, show your love to a woman loved by someone else, who has been unfaithful to you. In the same way the LORD loves the people of Israel, even though they worship other gods and love to eat the raisin cakes" (Hosea 3:1 NCV).

Forgiveness is not a feeling; it is a choice, a deliberate action and an independent act between God and us. To forgive means to cancel the debt or send it away. In one traditional society, when someone pays a debt they owe, the loan paper is marked "Paid in Full" and then nailed above the door of their home for everyone to see. Forgiveness makes the choice to cancel the debt before the sandpaper person ever asks for forgiveness...or even if they never ask for forgiveness.

Gomer didn't ask for forgiveness. Like the children of Israel, she was sitting in her sin and eating raisin cakes, the pastry delicacies used by the pagans in their worship of the false god Baal. Some sandpaper people simply love being sandpaper people. Obviously, Gomer "loved adultery" and seemed happy in her sin. None of that mattered to Hosea. What did matter were obedience and the fulfillment of his commitment to God and to his wife. He forgave her and brought her home—again. When I first read the story of Hosea and Gomer, I could not for the life of me figure out why Hosea would do such a thing instead of telling this woman to hit the road! That's what I would have done in his place. But he was more concerned with pleasing God than pleasing others or satisfying his own wants and needs. Notice that he didn't bring her back with the attitude of "I have to do this or I will be in trouble with God." Hosea brought his unfaithful wife home to forgive her and love her. Personally, I thought God was asking an awful lot of him. But then, God can ask a lot because He gave a lot.

ove that chooses forgiveness is the only choice that sets us free from the chains of anger, resentment, revenge, and bitterness.

Forgiveness is the deepest need of our soul and God's greatest gift. The apostle Paul sent a life-changing message when he wrote this celebratory declaration of divine forgiveness: "God made you alive with Christ. He forgave all our sins. He canceled the record that contained the charges against us. He took it and destroyed it by nailing it to Christ's cross" (Colossians 2:13-14 NLT). Forgiveness must be given in the same proportion it is received. There should be no limits to our forgiveness, because there are no limits to the forgiveness of God. We can stop forgiving when we run out of His forgiveness. Instead, though, we stop forgiving when we run out of patience. When you really think about it, forgiveness is a radical choice, demanding radical action on our part.

A man was reemployed at a place he had been fired from several months earlier because of his poor performance on the job. This time, his work was outstanding. Remembering his earlier performance, a co-worker asked, "What happened?" In response to the question, the man told his story. "In college, I was part of a fraternity initiation committee. We took new members and placed them in the middle of a deserted country road. My job was to drive my car as fast as I could, straight toward them. They had to stand still until someone gave the signal they could jump out of the way! One dark night, I was driving 100 miles an hour. The signal was given and everyone jumped out of the way except for one boy who stood, frozen in fear.

"I left college, married, and had two children. But the face of that boy as I drove over him was in front of me every minute of every day! I became moody, inconsistent in my work, and finally began to drink heavily, hoping to numb the pain. As a result, my wife was forced to work long hours to support our family.

"One morning I was home alone—drinking—when the doorbell rang. When I opened the door, I stood face-to-face with the mother of the boy I had killed. 'I hated you for years,' she began. 'I spent long nights planning ways to get revenge. Then I met Jesus Christ, and He has filled my life with love and forgiveness. I came here today to let you know I forgive you and to ask you to forgive me.'" The man summed up his story by saying, "That forgiveness has changed my whole life."

Sandpaper people come in all grits. Sometimes they're just annoying or bothersome. It's easy to forgive them because there really is not much to forgive. However, there will be those very difficult relationships—sandpaper people of the coarsest possible grit, who can break our heart and destroy our world if we let them. We have a choice. We always have a choice to make when confronted with pain of this magnitude. Love that chooses forgiveness is the only choice that sets us free from the chains of anger, resentment, revenge, and bitterness. Right now, choose to forgive your sandpaper person—and you will find *your* heart set free as well.

CHOICE 3: CHOOSE TO SACRIFICE

I bought her for six ounces of silver and ten bushels of barley (Hosea 3:2 NCV)

Remember that Hosea was the one who had been wronged and humiliated. Yes, he was the one following God, but he was also the one called to sacrifice. I must admit that this calling goes against everything I think is just and fair—which is exactly the reason we are called to make the same sacrifices Hosea had to make. Sacrifice is the backbone of a love that refuses to give up and is the underlying support of our dealings with sandpaper people.

We misunderstand the full meaning of sacrifice, thinking that it is only a decision to "give up" self-centered rights, hoarded resources, or the freedom to walk away from difficult relationships. Beyond this, sacrifice is a mirror reflecting our own pride and sin, calling us to lay down all sense of human justice or fairness in order for God to work in and through us to love sandpaper people. What sacrifices did God call Hosea to make? We need to know because they are the same sacrifices God calls us to make in order to love that unlovable person God has allowed to come our way.

Hosea Sacrificed His Pride

The phrase "loved by another" suggests Gomer was owned by a family friend or fellow citizen. She may very well have been sleeping with one or more of Hosea's friends, or at the least, one of his neighbors. Hosea had to swallow his pride and go to her in love and forgiveness. Now let me just tell you, if I had been the one going to find Gomer, I would have snatched her up by the hair and dragged her home in front of as many people as possible in order to prove she could not get away with what she was doing. More likely, I would have said, "Good riddance. You can keep her!"

I am certain many would agree with my plan of punishment and revenge. It seems to me Hosea stood to gain very little but lose a great deal by choosing to respond as he did. He was to sacrifice everything in order to redeem a woman who didn't deserve any sacrifice or redemption. But then, that is exactly what Jesus Christ did on the cross for each one of us. Now He calls us to respond with a God-like heart attitude of redemption. Hosea chose to sacrifice his pride and forfeit all of his rights to provide restitution for his wife. God always honors a humble heart, a heart willing to crucify pride and choose humility.

Hosea Sacrificed His Rights

Even though Gomer was Hosea's wife, she broke the covenant of marriage. Don't miss this pivotal truth. Biblically, Hosea had every justification to divorce her, toss her out, and turn her children against her, stripping her life of every good thing. He could have destroyed her and no one would have blamed him. Instead, he laid down his anger, hurt, and right to retaliate or seek revenge.

It doesn't stop there, though. Hosea took the initiative and went to her! Matthew describes a forgiveness we find hard to understand: "If you are standing before the altar in the Temple, offering a sacrifice to God, and you suddenly remember that someone has something against you, leave your sacrifice there beside the altar. Go and be reconciled to that person. Then come and offer your sacrifice to God" (Matthew 5:23 NLT).

I believe this verse indicates that, if we know someone has something against us and we refuse to make things right, nothing we do or say will count in kingdom work. God always seeks restoration and reconciliation. He commands us to look past what seems like a logical reaction and look to the highest obedience we can offer.

Hosea Sacrificed His Money

Hosea had to buy back his own wife. Gomer was damaged goods, and she definitely wasn't on sale! Six ounces of silver and ten bushels of barley was the going price of a slave—and since prophets are definitely not in the top income bracket, the payment was a great financial sacrifice! Gomer's own sin had placed her in bondage. Even so, Hosea was willing to make a financial sacrifice in order to fulfill his commitment in marriage. Love that never gives up is willing to pay a price, to sacrifice so that people in bondage can be set free!

C.S. Lewis says it beautifully:

> To love at all is to be vulnerable. Love anything, and
> your heart will certainly be wrung and possibly be

broken. If you want to make sure of keeping it intact, you must give your heart to no one, not even to an animal…Lock it up safe in the casket or coffin of your selfishness. But in that casket—safe, dark, motionless, airless—it will change. It will not be broken; it will become unbreakable, impenetrable, and irredeemable. The only place outside of Heaven where you can be perfectly safe from all the dangers of love is Hell.[3]

Mother Teresa said, "Love, to be real, must cost! It must hurt! It must empty us of self!" The words of David reveal the essence of love and forgiveness: "King David answered… 'No, I must pay the full price. I won't take anything that is yours and give it to the Lord. I won't give an offering that costs me nothing'" (1 Chronicles 21:24 ICB).

Hosea could have played it safe. Gomer was not sorry! He had no guarantee she would not do the very same thing again. He took a huge risk in bringing his wife home! Can't you just hear his friends and family? "You deserve better, son." "I've been your friend for a long time, and I have to tell you this makes no sense." "I don't want to see you get hurt again." "Walk away from her, Hosea. Taking her back is a big mistake."

IN EVERY RELATIONSHIP, especially with sandpaper people, what passes for true love is often little more than a convenient emotional trade-off. Someone is kind to us, so we are kind in return. Someone treats us badly, so we don't get mad, we get even. Sound fair? Seem reasonable? Yes, but only in human terms, the terms under which difficult relationships operate. Love that never gives up goes beyond reason and refuses to settle for justice alone. Love that never gives up insists on granting mercy. The apostle Paul knew much about loving those who persecuted him because of his faith. In Ephesians 5:2 he writes, "Live a life of love, just as Christ loved us and gave himself up for us as a fragrant offering and sacrifice to

God." Any sacrifice made to Christ in the name of unfailing love is a sweet smelling offering to God!

A little boy's sister was near death, sick with the same disease from which he had recovered two years earlier. The doctor told him he could save his sister's life by giving her some of his blood. The hope was that, since the brother had survived, his blood would carry the antibodies that would now save his sister. On top of that, both children had a rare blood type. Her only chance seemed to be a transfusion from her brother. "Adam, are you sure you want to give your blood for Chrissy?" the doctor asked. The boy hesitated for several moments; his lips trembled as tears filled his eyes and a silent battle against fear ensued. His parents and the doctor assured him that the procedure would not be very painful and would be over with quickly. Finally, he smiled bravely and said, "Sure, Doctor. I'll give my blood for my sister." As brother and sister were wheeled into an empty operating room, neither one spoke; but when their eyes met, Adam grinned.

As the transfusion took place, the little girl began to respond immediately. It was working—she would live! Parents, doctors, and nurses erupted into cheers and applause. When the ordeal was almost over, Adam's brave little voice was heard—"Say, Doctor—when do I die?" A stunned silence fell on the room. It was only then the doctor and parents realized why the little boy had hesitated, why he had cried earlier. Adam had thought that when he gave his blood to his sister, he would die. Love that never gives up is willing to pay a great price and make a great sacrifice! Love that never gives up can transform a sandpaper person into a velvet person. Love that never gives up is yours to give.

CHOICE 4: CHOOSE TO RESTORE

I told her, "You must wait for me for many days. You must not be a prostitute, and you must not have sexual relations with any other man. I will act the same way toward you" (Hosea 3:3 NCV).

When Hosea brought Gomer home, he demonstrated love and forgiveness by standing firm in his commitment to her and to trying again. He fixed his eyes and heart on restoration, not condemning his wife, but rather her behavior. Just as God separates us from our sin, He calls us to do the same with sandpaper people. We must separate who they are from their actions, loving the sinner but hating the sin, looking beyond their faults to see their needs.

Most people I know find restoration not only painful to endure, but extremely difficult to practice with sandpaper people. Sandpaper people know little about restoration because few people are willing to take the time and spend the energy it takes to hold them accountable for their behavior. It is much easier to chalk their abrasiveness up to a flawed character, an abhorrent attitude, or just plain meanness—without taking the time to look deeper in order to address the reasons behind their actions. Sandpaper people are the walking wounded, in dire need of restoration and healing. Restoration always demands an emotional and spiritual investment that permeates every part of the relationship.

Hosea wanted to restore his marriage; but he first wanted to restore Gomer. He was willing to hold his wife accountable, setting aside his own needs for the higher purpose of restoration. His motives were pure and steeped in love. Our motives must be pure and loving as well when it comes to holding our sandpaper person accountable. It is easy to falsify accountability, using it as an opportunity to vent frustration and, if we are brutally honest, even hold onto a hint of revenge. True accountability must focus on nothing short of complete restoration.

CHOICE 5: CHOOSE TO LOVE THE WAY GOD LOVES

> In the same way Israel will live many days without a
> king or leader, without sacrifices or holy stone pillars,
> and without the holy vest or an idol. After this, the
> people of Israel will return to the LORD their God and

follow him and the king from David's family. In the
last days they will turn in fear to the LORD, and he will
bless them (Hosea 3:4-5 NCV).

The marriage of Hosea and Gomer is meant to be a picture of
our relationship with God, illustrating His unwavering love for us,
His children. Like Gomer, we have been unfaithful to God. We
have become prostitutes of this world, depending on the wrong
people and the wrong things, selling ourselves to unworthy desires
and goals. We have run from our faithful God and His precious
love nailed to the cross, straight into the arms of our own inade-
quacies and selfish desires. We have even followed after false gods,
filling our lives and hearts with the clutter of people and things we
worship instead of worshiping the one true God. But we must face
the stark reality that anything or anyone who stands between God
and us is an idol!

Like Gomer, we have become comfortable in our sin, compla-
cent in a disobedient lifestyle. In fact, we are quick to lavish condemnation on Gomer while we cherish and cling to our own pet
sins; but just as Hosea loved Gomer, God loves us unconditionally,
right in the middle of our ruin and waste. Our hope and deliver-
ance is found in Him alone: "God shows his great love for us in
this way: Christ died for us while we were still sinners" (Romans
5:8 NCV). The name "Hosea" means "salvation," and just like
Hosea was Gomer's salvation, God is ours. He looks past our
rebellious hearts filled with unfaithfulness and pursues us still.
Like Hosea, God is eternally committed to us, refusing to give up
until He brings us home. I love the words Paul uses as he cele-
brates the security of his relationship with God: "Whether we are
high above the sky or in the deepest ocean, nothing in all creation
will ever be able to separate us from the love of God that is
revealed in Christ Jesus our Lord" (Romans 8:39 NLT).

The parallel is clear. When it comes to dealing with difficult
people, we are to view and respond in the way Hosea responded to
Gomer, knowing that every difficult relationship we experience

comes for a reason—with God's permission and as part of His plan to refine and purify our hearts. It is through these sandpaper people that we grow and mature in Christ. The rough edges are smoothed away as we welcome the lessons these people bring; and into their lives God asks us to pour out His love, a love that never gives up and never fails.

> Love is patient.
> Love is kind.
> Love does not envy.
> Love is not easily angered.
> Love keeps no record of wrongs.
> Love never fails.
>   —Adapted from 1 Corinthians 13:4-5,8

SANDPAPER DREAMS

Psychologists say that seeing sandpaper in your dream suggests you need to smooth over some rough spots in your relationships and deal with petty irritations involving relatives or close friends. It may also indicate abrasiveness or harshness in your words or attitudes.

According to tradition, if your dreams feature scraping with metal, it portends a broken friendship. If they involve stone, it is a sign you will shortly have reason to be grateful to the good influences that surround you; scraping by sandpaper predicts some pleasant romantic news—possibly a wedding.[4]

Be Encouraging:
Become Their Cheerleader

*Encourage each other and
give each other strength.*
1 Thessalonians 5:11 NCV

ONE SECRET OF DEFUSING and disarming sandpaper people is to become their cheerleader. Notice, I didn't say we have to *feel* like being their cheerleader. We must choose to see them as God sees them, change our focus to their good points, and then voice them! A judge utters a few words and a guilty man is sentenced to death row. A friend speaks a word of encouragement and a desperate heart finds hope. A mother lashes out with angry words and the light in her child's eyes disappears. A wife offers a word of forgiveness and her marriage is restored. A gossip makes a phone call and a reputation is destroyed. A teenager says "yes" and changes the course of her life. The power of the spoken word is great. Sandpaper people are accustomed to being the target of harsh words. In fact, many of these difficult people delight in deliberately provoking words of criticism and condemnation in order to prove that what they really believe about themselves is true—they are broken and cannot be mended.

In a small country church, a novice altar boy serving the priest at Sunday mass accidentally dropped the glass of wine. The priest struck the boy, knocking him to the ground. Standing over him, the angry cleric shouted, "Get out and don't come back!" That boy became Tito, the Yugoslav Communist leader. In another cathedral in the heart of a city, a young altar boy serving the bishop at Sunday mass accidentally dropped the glass of wine. With a warm twinkle in his eyes, the bishop hugged the young boy to his side and gently whispered, "Someday you will be a wonderful priest." That boy grew up to become Archbishop Fulton Sheen.

Words can change the course of one's life, defusing anger and turning tragedy into triumph. Just as unkind words spoken over time, can create a sandpaper person, kind words spoken over time can radically impact the hearts and lives of difficult people. It is a paradox to me that those who most need encouragement and a cheer or two along the way are those who least deserve them—in our eyes. In the eyes of God, sandpaper people are the walking wounded—fumbling through life, looking for love in all the wrong places, trying to find acceptance and worth in all the wrong ways. Even though sandpaper people often live with tragedy and disaster perpetually simmering beneath the surface, the true cause for their rage is rarely seen. A heartbreaking childhood, a devastating loss, a shattered hope or broken relationship may feed their smoldering anger. If tragic and disastrous consequences don't erupt on their own, a sandpaper person will many times set into action a series of events that will surely provoke an eruption of some kind and then wait for the predictable and well-deserved verbal indictments to flow. With our words, though, we have the power to extinguish the source of those disparaging words. Proverbs 31:26 says it well—"She speaks wise words and teaches others to be kind" (NCV).

Words of Life

I will never forget the day I learned just how powerful words can be and how far-reaching their capability to teach and train is. My teachers in this lesson were the most abrasive person I have ever met and one of the kindest young girls ever to grace my life.

The first 13 years of our ministry saw Dan and me working with teenagers as youth pastors in three different churches. The youth we helped and served came primarily from homes that, at first glance, seemed healthy and whole. I quickly learned that outer trappings often masquerade inner ruin. A young man named Jack (names have been changed to protect the guilty) joined our youth group, having recently moved to the area because, as he put it, "My parents like to move a lot." That should have been my first clue.

In the beginning, Jack worked hard at making friends and seemed content to go with the flow—until the day he decided the stream of life was flowing in the wrong direction and it was up to him to redirect its course. The mask came off and the façade crumbled. Standing before me was the real deal, a genuine, authentic sandpaper person of the coarsest grit. It started with little things—a seemingly friendly shove, caustic comments masquerading as humor—and words of darkness and destruction grew into a constant stream. Other teenagers began coming to Dan or me, sharing their concern and eventually their disgust at Jack's antics. I talked to him. Dan talked to him. Together, we prayed for him and urged the others to join us. Reluctantly but faithfully, they began praying that Jack, the sandpaper person, would be transformed into Jack, the velvet person. Nothing changed. As a last-ditch effort, we drafted two of our most mature youth to take Jack under their wing and mentor him. Jack didn't want to be mentored, and the effort was in vain.

During one Monday-night Bible study, Dan asked one of those mentors to sing a solo. Jami was a redheaded, freckle-faced girl whose sparkling blue eyes and contagious dimpled grin did not convey the constant pain she suffered from juvenile rheumatoid arthritis. She never complained and always shared her faith in God and His goodness to her. Everyone loved her and the pure voice with which she sang. You *had* to love Jami. She was our litmus test for newcomers. If you didn't love Jami, there was obviously something wrong with you. Well, something was wrong with Jack.

As Jami stood to sing, Jack began laughing, pointing, and whispering to the people around him. Their lack of response fueled the fire, upping the ante. He had to win this degrading battle and capture center stage. With desperate and questioning eyes, Jami stared at me, silently begging me to rescue her and the situation. I smiled the most encouraging smile I could muster, hoping it would be enough. It wasn't. I looked back at Jack, delivering my famous and usually feared "shape up or die a horrible death" glare—all to no avail. Dan asked, "Jack, are you ready to hear Jami sing?" Well, that did it! Jack erupted into uproarious laughter, falling on his side as he spoke the words I was certain Jami would never forget. "Sing? Have you heard her sing? She sounds like a frog—not to mention the fact that she walks funny!" Every ounce of oxygen was instantaneously sucked out of the room. Everyone froze—except Jami, who fled in tears. From the faces of those sitting around Jack, I could tell that well-deserved revenge was close at hand as they began loading their emotional guns and gathering their mental weapons of retaliation. Wanting first shot at this obviously hateful and mean-spirited young man, I jumped to my feet, grabbed him by his ear (no, I am not kidding), and pulled him out of the room toward sure death.

Reaching the foyer, I whirled Jack around to face me and with clenched teeth ground out my accusation: "Do you have *any* idea what you just did?" The laughter vanished as pain and the harsh realization slowly spread across his face, his response was nothing short of incredible. "Yes. I embarrassed Jami and hurt her feelings." I'm not often speechless, but at that moment, words simply evaporated as I stared into the eyes of someone fully aware of the pain he had just inflicted on one of the few people who truly accepted and was forever defending him. I finally continued. "I cannot believe you! Jami has always been kind to you, coming to your defense when you didn't deserve to be defended, inviting you to join the group when no one wanted you anywhere around. She has probably been the best friend you've ever had or ever will have. What is wrong with you?" Jack stood there, silently accepting his rightful and, I thought, well-deserved punishment without a single word of defense.

From the corner of my eye, I saw someone approaching. I sincerely hoped they were bringing me some kind of sharp weapon! Instead, it was the one person God would use to eternally change Jack and set his feet on the road to wholeness. It was Jami, a tremulous smile breaking through the tears cascading down her face. Jack instinctively began backing away, until he saw her eyes and the outstretched arms she offered him. In astonishment, I stood paralyzed, a witness to God's supernatural presence and the restorative power of forgiveness at work before my unbelieving eyes and my angry heart.

Instantly, I became the student and Jami the teacher. Both Jack and I listened quietly as God spoke through this precious young woman the words only she had the right to speak. "Jack, I got to thinking about why you did what you just did. I realized something. I love you and you know that. But you don't think you deserve that love, so you tried to kill it by hurting me. It won't work. Do you know why?" Sitting at the feet of this wise-beyond-her-years master teacher, I saw Jack's sandpaper world being rocked by a love he couldn't understand and was fully convinced he didn't deserve—a love that was not altered by anything he did or didn't do, a love that only God can give. In answer to Jami's question, he gave a quick shake of head and whispered, "No. I don't know why." Jami smiled, wrapped her arms around the very one who, just moments before, had viciously wounded her, and with fresh tears streaming down her face, choked out words I will never forget. "I love you with God's love, Jack. Not mine. And His love just won't die. People tried to kill it on the cross, but even that didn't work. So I just wanted to tell you that I love you—no matter what you say or do. I am your friend—period."

Staring into her eyes, I imagine Jack experienced, maybe for the first time, the ageless and stubborn love of God—an overwhelming love that literally redefined him and the man he would become. With a giggle, Jami playfully grabbed his hand and, pulling him toward the place of forgiveness that only her love could take him, chattered happily about how she needed him on the front row to encourage her while she sang. He did!

That isn't the end of the story. From that day forward, Jack was a different person—not perfect, but different. From time to time, he would fall back into old emotional habits. When he did, Jami or someone under her direction and influence would snatch him back to the new place where words of staggering kindness and God ordained wisdom had brought him. The youth who witnessed Jami's love for this unlovable one even when it didn't make sense and was completely undeserved, were changed and called higher in their obedience to God.

When it comes to dealing with sandpaper people, one crucial discipline of encouragement stands out from all the rest—learning to control the tongue. There are certain verbal responses sandpaper people expect when rubbing someone the wrong way. Personally, this is an area of great struggle for me when it comes to dealing with the difficult relationships in my life. I tend to spout formulas, sermons, edicts, and ultimatums in order to control the irritating person who is trying to control and manipulate me. It never works. What does work—what can we do to control our tongue?

STEP 1: UNDERSTAND THAT THE TONGUE IS A GIFT FROM GOD

To man belong the plans of the heart, but from the LORD comes the reply of the tongue (Proverbs 16:1).

The gift of communication comes from God! The sad reality of a sandpaper person's life is that while they long for someone who will communicate with them on a heart basis, their actions tend to drive away the very people who would be willing to do so. Sandpaper people are poor communicators because they depend upon the tainted and inadequate heart motives of mankind in order to understand the true meaning behind others' words. On the other hand, God sweeps aside the pretense and bravado to expose their raw need. To communicate with the abrasive people in our lives requires spiritual intervention and authentic interpretation of a sandpaper person's needs and wants. In other words, God must be the translator between our heart and the heart of those people we find difficult.

In difficult relationships, the ability to communicate clearly is an essential tool but also one of the hardest to master. I love the story of a woman who made an appointment with a marriage counselor. "Why are you here today?" the counselor asked. "I want to divorce my husband!" she explained in no uncertain terms. The counselor continued, "Do you have any grounds?" The woman paused for a moment before responding. "Yes, almost an acre." The slightly amused counselor answered, "I'm sorry. I wasn't clear. Do you and your husband have a grudge match?" A confused look spread across the woman's face as she answered, "Actually we don't, but we do have a nice carport. Frankly, though, that is a silly question and has nothing to do with the fact that I want a divorce." The exasperated counselor shook his head and closed the file on his desk. "Ma'am, I'm sorry! But, in my professional opinion, I see no reason why you should divorce your husband!" Grabbing her purse and jumping to her feet, the woman headed for the door, declaring with irritation, "It's clear to me you have no idea what you are doing, talking about land and our garage, of all things. Why, you are just like my husband. The man just cannot carry on an intelligent conversation!" Sandpaper people find communication complex, and they are often misunderstood, resulting in emotional walls and a skewed emotional balance. If the sandpaper person cannot control his or her tongue, then we must control ours.

While the tongue is a gift from God, it is our responsibility to manage and use that gift of communication for good. Growth, accountability, encouragement, strength, and support are the rewards of time and energy invested in healthy and right communication. It's in relationships that much of who we are is realized.

A teacher asked each of her students to list the names of the other students, leaving a space between each name. She then told them to think of the nicest thing they could say about each of their classmates and write it down. The teacher recorded the name of each student on a separate sheet of paper, listing what everyone else said about that individual. She gave each student his or her list. Before long, the entire class was smiling. "Really?" she heard whispered. "I never knew that I meant anything to anyone!" and, "I didn't know others liked me so much" were most of the comments. No one ever mentioned those papers in class again. The teacher never knew if they discussed them after class or with their parents, but it didn't matter. The exercise had accomplished its purpose. The students were happy with themselves and one another. That group of students moved on.

Years later, one of the students was killed in Vietnam, and his teacher attended his funeral. The church was packed with his friends and, one by one, they filed by the coffin. The teacher was the last one to come. As she stood there, one of the soldiers who acted as pallbearer came up to her. "Were you Mark's math teacher?" he asked. She nodded. Then he said, "Mark talked about you a lot."

After the funeral, most of Mark's former classmates went together to a luncheon. Mark's mother and father were there, obviously waiting to speak with his teacher. "We want to show you something," his father said, taking a wallet out of his pocket. "They found this on Mark when he was killed. We thought you might recognize it." Opening the billfold, he carefully removed two worn pieces of notebook paper that had obviously been taped, folded, and refolded many times. The teacher knew without looking that the papers were the ones on which she had listed all the good things each of Mark's classmates had said about him. "Thank you so much for doing that," Mark's mother said. "As you can see, he treasured it."

Mark's former classmates gathered around. Carl smiled rather sheepishly and said, "I still have my list in my desk at home." Chuck's wife said, "Chuck put his in our wedding album." "I have mine too," Marilyn said. "It's in my diary." Then Vicki, another classmate, reached into her purse, took out her wallet, and showed her worn and tattered list to the group. "I always carry this with me," she said. Without batting an eyelash, she added: "I think we all saved our lists." The teacher finally sat down and cried as she realized that what you put into the lives of others comes back into your own. And when those deposits are encouraging words, they live on and reap eternal harvests.

In the life of most sandpaper people, there is a lack of positive emotional deposits. They have never had a cheerleader nor do they feel they deserve one. When we deposit words of truth and love, patience and acceptance, their emotional balance moves into the black and a healthy relationship can begin.

STEP 2: RECOGNIZE THE POWER OF THE TONGUE

> What you say affects how you live. You will be rewarded by how you speak. What you say can mean life or death. Those who speak with care will be rewarded (Proverbs 18:20-21 ICB).

The manager of a megastore came to check on his new salesman at the end of his first day. "How many customers did you have today?" he asked. "One," replied the new guy. "Only one?" said the boss. "For how much?" The salesman pulled out his copy of the receipt for the day and proudly answered, "$58,334." "What?" the manager asked, thinking the young man had to be mistaken. Seeing his boss's expression, the novice repeated, "I really did sell him $58,334 worth of merchandise." The manager was amazed and asked the young man to explain. "Well, it really was easy. First, I sold the man a fishhook, then a rod and reel. When I asked him where he planned to fish, he said he was headed down the coast. I suggested he would need a boat, so he bought a 20-footer but then realized his car wasn't powerful enough to pull it, so I sold him an SUV." The boss listened in stunned silence. "You sold all that to a guy who came in for a fishhook?" "No, sir," the young salesman replied. "He actually came in for a bottle of aspirin because his wife had a headache. I told him that since his weekend was already shot, he might as well go fishing."

> ith just two words—"meat loaf"—my husband suggests it might be a good night to eat out! Words affect lives!

Words are persuasive, powerful, and eternal, marching through the years, living forever in the heart and soul of the person to whom they are spoken. In what I believe to be one of the strongest passages found in the Bible, James describes the great power of the tongue. "We all make many mistakes, but those who control their tongues can also control themselves in every other way" (James 3:2 NLT). If we can control our tongue, we can control our lives.

With just two words—"meat loaf"—my husband suggests it might be a good night to eat out, the kids race to the car, ready and willing to eat anywhere, and I am one happy camper! Words affect lives! James says it well: "We can make a large horse turn around and go wherever we want by means of a small bit in its mouth. And a tiny rudder makes a huge ship turn wherever the pilot wants it to go, even though the winds are strong" (James 3:3-4 NLT). James compares the tongue to a bit in the mouth of a horse and to the rudder of a ship, two things that are small but exercise great power—just like the tongue. A small bit enables the rider to control the whole horse just as a small rudder enables the pilot to steer a large ship. A life can change direction simply because a few pointed words are spoken. The bit and the rudder must be under the control of a strong hand to accomplish what they were created to accomplish. So must the tongue. When God controls our tongue, He controls us. Never underestimate the guidance you give or the direction your life takes because of the words you speak or refuse to speak.

Relationship-Building

The tongue builds or destroys relationships. Every healthy relationship is built upon the words we speak, the words we don't speak, the way we say them, and the time and place we choose to say them. Paul warns, "Do not let any unwholesome talk come out of your mouths, but only what is helpful for building others up according to their needs" (Ephesians 4:29). Most sandpaper people have built such thick defenses around their hearts that the use or misuse of words matters little to them—which is one reason they cannot seem to make or keep lasting friendships. Words are important building blocks of healthy relationships. When we choose to use words of encouragement in dealing with sandpaper people, we are inviting God to work in and through our spoken words to strengthen and build healthier relationships.

When the little boy asked his dad to play darts, his directions to his father were simple. "I'll throw the darts, and you say 'wonderful.'" With words of encouragement, I can deposit courage into a heart and life. Paul reminds us of this striking truth in 1 Thessalonians 5:11: "Encourage each other and give each other strength" (NCV). One of the greatest ways we can encourage and give each other strength is through words!

Several years ago, we bought a small ski boat and began teaching both of our kids how to water-ski. Our son, Jered, went first. A natural athlete, he was soon up and skiing around the entire lake. Then it was Danna's turn. Earlier in the day, she had broken a toe and decided that putting that swollen and painful toe in a tight-fitting water-ski boot was just too much to ask. I was totally sympathetic, but her brother and dad were convinced she needed to learn how to ski—immediately.

Her next excuse was that the lake was filled with alligators just waiting for her to fall and make her the star of the six-o'clock news as the reptiles' favorite snack. Dan and Jered didn't buy that excuse either and patiently explained that since we were in upper New York state, the likelihood of encountering an alligator was slim to none. It seemed to me that they were rather narrow-minded in their rationale; nevertheless, into the water Danna went, skis on, fuming with anger and awaiting her tragic fate. Ignoring her protests, Dan gave detailed instructions on what to do in order to get up on her skis. He gunned the motor and pulled her halfway out of the water. She, however, preferred to stay in the watery half. After falling several times and swallowing a significant amount of lake water, she was ready to quit—until her brother said, "Danna, you can do this! I'm going to help you." With that, he jumped in the water, patiently helping her retrieve and reposition her skis, encouraging her the whole time. On the next try, she popped out of the water and skied around the entire lake like a pro! Sometimes, all it takes is a word of encouragement to make the difference between success and failure, or defuse an emotional bomb tossed our way by that person who rubs us the wrong way.

Relationship-Destroying

Proverbs tells us that "reckless words pierce like a sword, but the tongue of the wise brings healing" (12:18). Careless words launched without forethought constitute reckless action and an irresponsible use of the tongue. Sandpaper people are pros at speaking before thinking and seem to delight in pushing any button that will provoke the same response in us. An even more frightening reality is that rash speaking can easily turn anyone into a sandpaper person. I often find my mouth is in motion before my brain is in gear. As a result, hearts are pierced and wounds are inflicted, the perfect setting for the emergence of a sandpaper person. We need to think before we speak. Healing words will come if we do.

Right now, your heart is probably aching at the memory of ugly words spoken by a sandpaper person in your life. Time really doesn't correct the sins of the tongue. Spoken words can never be "unspoken." We can confess each harsh word we speak and even be forgiven by others for speaking them, but the fire stoked by abrasive words still burns and destroys. Healing will come, in God's time and by His hand.

A seminary student named Sally relates an experience in her Bible class, which was taught by a Dr. Smith, who was known for his elaborate object lessons. The minute she walked into the classroom one day, she knew she was in for fun. On the wall was a big target, and on a nearby table were many darts. Dr. Smith told the students to draw a picture of someone they disliked; he would allow them to throw darts at the picture. One student drew a picture of a girl who had stolen her boyfriend. Another drew a picture of his little brother. Sally drew a picture of a former friend, putting in a great deal of detail, down to pimples on her face. She was pleased at the overall effect she had achieved.

The class lined up and began throwing darts with great laughter and hilarity. Some threw their darts with such force that their targets were ripping apart. Sally was looking forward to her turn but was disappointed when Dr. Smith called time and asked the students to return to their seats. As she sat there thinking about how angry she was because she hadn't had a chance to throw any darts, Dr. Smith began removing the target from the wall. Underneath was a picture of Jesus. A complete hush fell over the room as each student viewed the mangled picture. Holes and jagged marks covered His face and pierced His eyes of love. Dr. Smith said only these words: "Inasmuch as ye have done it unto the least of these my brethren, ye have done it unto me" (Matthew 25:40 KJV). No other words were necessary; the tear-filled eyes of each student focused only on the face of Christ. Destructive words are verbal darts we tend to aim at sandpaper people. When they find their mark, ruin is the result. But under God's control, words build solid relationships.

STEP 3: LEARN TO CONTROL THE TONGUE

> He who guards his lips guards his life, but he who speaks rashly will come to ruin (Proverbs 13:3).

If we don't learn to use and control our tongue, it will use and control us! How can we learn to manage our mouth and control our tongue?

Check Your Heart

> The mouth speaks the things that are in the heart. Good people have good things in their hearts, and so they say good things. But evil people have evil in their hearts, so they say evil things (Matthew 12:34-35 NCV).

The relationship between man's heart and his tongue is direct. In other words, what's down in the well comes up in the bucket, especially when that bucket is being yanked to the surface by someone who rubs us the wrong way. When you squeeze an orange, you get orange juice. When a sandpaper person puts the "squeeze" on our emotions, what's really inside will come out. Boastful words come from an insecure heart and filthy words from an impure heart. Critical words flow freely from a bitter heart, while painful heart wounds produce stinging words. The problem is not my mouth. The problem is my heart. The writer of Proverbs agrees: "A wise man's heart guides his mouth" (16:23). In other words, what is inside our heart will eventually work its way out in our character. When Jesus Christ is the Lord of the heart, He is Lord of the lips as well.

During my annual checkup, the doctor came into the examining room and did what he always does first. He asked me to stick out my tongue. Over the years, I have had countless exams, and almost every doctor has asked to see my tongue at some point during their examination. It had never occurred to me to question the procedure—until this particular moment. I had to ask. "Why is it important for you to examine my tongue? Do you have extra little wooden sticks to use up or are you stalling for time?" He laughed and responded with a surprising explanation. "The health of the tongue is a strong indicator of how healthy the whole body is."

As his words sank in, I was struck by the truth that if there is something wrong with my words, I need to examine my heart for the reason. I love this verse found in Proverbs 10:20: "The tongue of the righteous is choice silver, but the heart of the wicked is of little value." The control of the tongue begins with an obedient heart, a heart committed to truth, a heart under the control of the Holy Spirit. We don't need to turn over a new leaf—we need a new life. Ezekiel 18:31 plainly says, "Clean house. No more rebellions, clean house. No more rebellions, please. Get a new heart!" (MSG). A personal relationship with Jesus Christ gives us a new heart, the clean heart needed to effectively deal with difficult people.

Guard Your Mind

> Test me, O LORD, and try me, examine my heart and my mind (Psalm 26:2).

In Darby's Bible translation, "mind" is rendered "reins," which is the old-fashioned word for *guts*—that is, the seat of our feelings. But it also makes us think of the fact that our mind "holds the reins" of our tongue. The heart, the mind, and the tongue cannot be separated. In Psalm 19:14 we read, "May the words of my mouth and the thoughts of my heart be pleasing to you, O LORD, my rock and my redeemer" (NLT). At times our mind goes blank but we forget to turn off the sound! The bridle for our tongue is a controlled thought life. Paul agrees when he writes, "We demolish arguments and every pretension that sets itself up against the knowledge of God, and we take captive every thought to make it obedient to Christ" (2 Corinthians 10:5).

My son is the starting running back on his college football team. He has played football for years and loves the game, especially the hitting and scoring-touchdowns part. However, he does not like the constant bombardment of foul language he must endure. I once asked Jered, "Son, how can I pray for you?" His answer was hilarious but also insightful. "Mom, just pray that I can tackle the garbage in my mind before it runs over my tongue and out of my mouth." Guarding the mind means tackling the garbage, tossing it out before it contaminates the words we speak. Guarding the mind means setting the parameters for dealing with sandpaper people *before* we are required to deal with sandpaper people. The guard must be in place before the battle begins.

Ask God for Help

> Take control of what I say, O Lord and keep my lips sealed (Psalm 141:3 NLT).

Trying to control our tongues on our own is a losing proposition. In fact, it is impossible—without the supernatural power of God. James 1:26 makes it clear that the control of the tongue is initiated by a heart committed to God. "If anyone considers himself religious and yet does not keep a tight rein on his tongue, he deceives himself and his religion is worthless." Simply put, if God is not in control of our tongue, our "religion" is nothing more than a set of lifeless, impotent rules.

A young husband was watching a beautiful but clearly distraught baby while his wife was shopping. Even though the infant was screaming, the father seemed to be completely in control. Gently rocking it, he whispered repeatedly, "Easy now, Andrew. Hold your temper." A woman passing by remarked, "You're a wonderful father to little Andrew! You seem to know just how to speak to a baby." "Baby nothing!" was his frustrated reply. "*My* name is Andrew!" Asking God to take control of our tongue is like stationing a guard at a city gate to keep watch. He is there by invitation only, an invitation we must deliberately choose to issue. We must ask God to help us control our tongue.

Speak Less

> Do not be quick with your mouth, do not be hasty in your heart to utter anything before God. God is in heaven and you are on earth, so let your words be few (Ecclesiastes 5:2 NCV).

There is a reason God gave us two ears but only one mouth. We need to listen more and talk less! I have discovered that saving face is often accomplished by keeping the lower part of it shut! Albert Einstein was the guest of honor at a dinner given for him by the president of Swarthmore College. When called on to give a speech, Einstein stunned the audience with his reply: "Ladies and gentlemen, I'm very sorry, but I have nothing to say." Then he sat down. A few seconds later, he stood back up and said, "When I do have something to say I'll come back." Six months later, he wrote the president, "Now I have something to say!" Another dinner was held and he made a speech!

If we never said anything unless we knew what we were talking about, a tremendous hush would descend upon the earth. What we don't say never has to be explained. A closed mouth gathers no feet. Matthew 12:36 is unforgettably pointed in its warning—"On the Judgment Day people will be responsible for every careless thing they have said" (NCV). We would be wise to speak less!

Words are a powerful gift from God, but every gift comes with the responsibility to use that gift in the right way! Every sandpaper person in your life will, at one time or another, hurl scathing words at you, hoping to snap your self-control like a sharp blade slashes through a tightly strung cord. If you respond with the same kind of abusive words, they win. Look behind those harsh words for the wound that caused them, and choose words of restoration. Listen not only to what sandpaper people say, but to what they don't say as well.

When Jered was in second grade, one of his classmates definitely qualified as a first-class sandpaper person. No one liked the boy for one simple reason—he was obnoxious and irritating. One Monday morning, he came to school with both arms in a cast from wrist to elbow. Over the weekend, he had fallen out of a tree and fractured both arms. The teacher stood with the anxious mother, explaining that the boy would need a friend to help him if he was to continue school. This friend would help the injured boy with his class assignments, feed him lunch, take him to the restroom, carry his books and, in short, be his personal slave for eight weeks.

When the teacher explained the situation to her students, tension filled the classroom. Not a word was spoken. No one moved. No one met the teacher's gaze. It seemed as if everyone was holding their breath, desperately hoping this circumstance would somehow disappear. It didn't. As the disappointed teacher finally turned to the woman, whose son was clearly unwanted and disliked, Jered stood up and said, "I'll do it, Miss Chism." A sigh of relief was heard as everyone stared at my son in gratitude. Jered has always been easygoing and well-liked, and he usually has a large group of friends around him. Though his classmates couldn't understand why he would deliberately link himself to this thoroughly unlikable kid, they were clearly glad he had.

Over the next eight weeks, Jered discovered this boy was not so bad after all. In fact, they became friends, and amazing changes occurred. The boy's behavior began to change because, if Jered liked him, there must be something in him to like. Jered began to encourage him and speak words of kindness to this unkind boy. Even when he responded in anger, Jered ignored that anger and continued to encourage him.

The other children watched day after day as this unlikely friendship unfolded, eventually also deciding that if Jered liked the sandpaper boy, there must be something worth liking. By the end of the eight weeks, the class of now wiser children was taking care of the boy and including him in every activity. When the casts came off, so did the old broken sandpaper person this boy had once been. All he had needed was a cheerleader. Maybe that's all your sandpaper person needs.

SANDPAPER CLOTHES

Sandpaper jeans. Use sandpaper on some key spots: the knees, back pockets, top of waistband, and any other area you want to look a little distressed. Rub vigorously. Sandpaper works especially well on darker washes.

Then pick another spot and give it tiny snips with scissors. Use a razor blade to pick at the tear, making it looked frayed without looking cut from a pattern.

Sandpaper slacks. A tongue-in-cheek method to abrade your way to smoother legs—use sandpaper-lined slacks. They can also be turned inside out to make snow angels on hardwood floors. (Just kidding!)

Five

Be Patient:
Learn to Endure

The Lord's servants must...
be patient with difficult people.
2 Timothy 2:24 NLT

IT TOOK 22 YEARS FOR the McDonald's hamburger chain to make its first billion dollars. It took IBM 46 years and Xerox 63 years to make the first billion. Harvey Mackay, in his book *Swim with the Sharks*, tells of an interview with the 88-year-old president of Japan's largest and most successful electrical enterprise.

> Q: Mr. President, does your company have long-range goals?
>
> A: Yes.
>
> Q: How long are your long-range goals?
>
> A: 250 years.
>
> Q: What do you need to carry them out?
>
> A: Patience.

When it comes to getting along with people who rub you the wrong way, patience is vital. Sandpaper people seem to have the uncanny ability to sense when patience is running low, seizing the opportunity to attack. Patience robs a sandpaper person of the satisfaction gained from pushing the most sensitive emotional buttons they can locate in the lives of those around them. Instead of trying to control sandpaper people, we must be patient, because patience is more powerful and more valuable than control can ever be. "It is better to be patient than powerful. It is better to win control over yourself than over whole cities" (Proverbs 16:32 GNT). A patient person is a powerful person. Patience comes from within and is not dependent upon external circumstances. Patience is the capacity to endure because of a controlled *inner* strength. The question is, how do we unleash the power of patience in our lives?

STEP 1: RECOGNIZE GOD AS THE SOURCE OF PATIENCE

In Romans 15:5, Paul clearly notes, "Patience and encouragement come from God" (NCV). Patience is rooted in and flows from the heart of God. It is in a personal relationship with God that we experience the power of patience and the strength to go on, even in the midst of a relationship storm. "God will strengthen you with his own great power so that you will not give up when troubles come, but you will be patient" Colossians 1:11 (NCV). God is the power supply for patience, enabling us to love those hard-to-love people! His part in the process of patience being cultivated *in* us is to make His patience available *to* us. Let's take a look at the two ways in which He does this.

Through the Bible

The Scriptures give us patience (Romans 15:4 NCV).

A group of four-year-old children were gathered in a Bible class. Their enthusiastic teacher asked, "Does anyone know what today is?" A little girl held up her hand and said, "It's Palm Sunday!" "Fantastic!" the teacher exclaimed. "Now, does anyone know what next Sunday is?" The same little girl held up her hand and said, "Yes, it's Easter Sunday." The teacher was thrilled. "That's great! Now does anyone know what makes next Sunday Easter?" Again, the same little girl responded with confidence, "Yes, next Sunday is Easter because Jesus rose from the grave." Before the teacher could congratulate the child on her knowledge of the Bible, the little girl quickly added, "But if He sees His shadow He has to go back in for seven weeks."

Many of us are like that little girl. We know just enough Scripture to get by, but when it comes right down to it, the Word of God has little impact on the everyday events of life. Dealing with sandpaper people requires wisdom beyond our own and strength we cannot muster. God promises to supply every need we have, and the main way He does that is through His Word. The psalmist says it well in Psalm 119:105: "Your word is a lamp for my feet and a light for my path" (ICB). When we regularly deposit the Word of God into our hearts and minds, it naturally works its way out in everyday life—adjusting attitudes, changing choices, altering actions, and revolutionizing relationships, especially those relationships we have with sandpaper people.

A Soviet official was asked why his country burned Bibles and punished those who dared to print and distribute them. His answer was profound. "We have discovered that the reading of the Bible changes people in a way that is dangerous to our cause!" The Word of God is the single most powerful tool we have in cultivating patience and impacting the way we deal with difficult relationships.

Through Our Circumstances

> Stay on the path that the LORD your God has commanded you to follow (Deuteronomy 5:33 NLT).

God transforms the paths we walk every day into spiritual classrooms in which we learn patience. Every relationship becomes the platform from which His unconditional love and unending patience is launched. It is that patience we must use when dealing with sandpaper people.

The people in my life who rub me the wrong way seem to have one characteristic in common—bad timing. It's amazing how many times a sandpaper person will show up at the worst possible moment, interrupting long-made plans with their demands for attention. We have a choice to make when sandpaper people intrude. We can allow those unwanted interruptions to scramble our emotions and stretch our nerves, or we can change our perspective. In Matthew 19:13 we find the patient response of Jesus to children who wanted to be with Him: "The people brought their little children to Jesus…his followers told them to stop, but Jesus said, 'Let the little children come to me. Don't stop them, because the kingdom of heaven belongs to people who are like these children'" (NCV). Sandpaper people so often remind me of children running from relationship to relationship and person to person in search of a safe place. God is calling us to be that safe place.

Life is not a series of accidents but a succession of divine appointments. That interruption we complain about, that intrusion we resent, is a window of opportunity sent by God! He uses the intrusive sandpaper person to rub off and sand away those attitudes and desires that are not wholly pleasing to Him. Like a well-sharpened scalpel, difficult relationships are God's tool to carve away the sinful mind-set that time is ours to arrange or spend and that relationships are ours to dictate. Our response to sandpaper people would drastically change if we adopted the perspective of building into every day's schedule margins of time that allow for divine interruptions.

Patience can also be found at the heart of every problem and trial. In fact, James encourages us to "consider it pure joy" when we "face trials of many kinds" (1:2 NLT). To "consider" is to lead our thinking, to rule our emotional reaction and steer our thoughts so we can respond to problems with joy, knowing that

God is in charge. Joy is the inner attitude that acknowledges the presence of God in the midst of the trial. We *will* have trials. Some of those trials will come as the result of dealing with difficult people. How we respond to sandpaper people partly depends on how patient we are. Patience empowers us to embrace that difficult person with an attitude of joy. I tend to consider it pure joy when I *escape*, rather than *embrace*, difficult people. It's clear from James that sandpaper people are not sent into our lives as punishment, but as opportunities for patience to work.

Endurance is a valuable lesson that can be learned at the feet of the most difficult relationship in your life. A typical bar of steel cut into ordinary reinforcing bar is doubled in value. Cut into needles, its value increases 70 times. That same bar of steel cut into delicate springs for watches increases in value by a factor of 50,000! The next time you encounter a sandpaper person, struggle with someone who rubs you the wrong way, or find yourself at the mercy of a difficult relationship, remember the bar of steel! Problems produce patience.

Relationships produce patience, too. The more difficult the relationship is, the more valuable the lesson. Proverbs 27:17 reveals one of the greatest gifts that sandpaper people bring to our lives: "As iron sharpens iron, so people can improve each other" (NCV). When a piece of iron is rubbed against another piece of iron, it shapes and sharpens both. The same is true in difficult relationships. When iron rubs against iron, sparks are sure to fly.

My daughter and I are exactly alike, which means we can easily push each other's buttons. I remember a particularly rough day filled with battles, none of which I seemed to win. My patience was wearing thin since everything I asked Danna to do was met with opposition and multiple reasons why she didn't want to comply with my wishes. I finally threw up my hands in total frustration, announcing, "Fine, Danna! Just do whatever you want. Now let me see you disobey that!" The absurdity of my words stopped me in my tracks, and I burst out laughing. The look of surprise on Danna's face was priceless, as was the lesson I learned that day. Pick your battles, and save your energy for important issues. The greatest patience is best refined in the midst of the greatest conflict. When conflicts come, use them, learn from them, and embrace them as a tool for good in the hands of God.

One of the most frustrating parts of any difficult relationship is the fact that sandpaper people seem to operate according to some schedule known only to them. As a result, we often find ourselves seated in one of God's waiting rooms, waiting for that exasperating person to become encouraging, hoping the difficult relationship with which we struggle will become easier. I hate to wait for anything or anyone—which is the very reason I am in God's waiting room to start with and the very purpose He has for the presence of sandpaper people in my life. They teach me to wait. It is in those waiting rooms that the condition of the heart is exposed. Who and what we really are emerge from the unique pressure only a difficult relationship can bring. "Remember how the LORD your God has led you in the desert for these forty years, taking away your pride and testing you, because he wanted to know what was in your heart" (Deuteronomy 8:2 NCV).

When we are patient and willing to wait on God, we are inviting Him to work. While we wait, He prepares us for that difficult relationship and fashions the difficult relationship to accomplish His plan in us. Difficult people barge into our lives with God's permission and by His design, invading forbidden territory and challenging cherished rules of our own making. When we become impatient, trying to run ahead of His work or escape those sandpaper people, we miss some of the blessings difficult relationships offer. It is through faith and patience that we obtain God's promises.

- The children of Israel waited 40 years to be delivered.
- Jesus waited 30 years to serve.
- Jeremiah waited 35 years for people to respond to his teaching.
- Abraham waited 70 years for a son.

Patience is trust—waiting! God is the source of patience and dispenses it through His word, our circumstances, and those "angels unaware" we call sandpaper people.

STEP 2: CHOOSE TO BE PATIENT

Be patient until the Lord comes again. A farmer patiently waits for his valuable crop to grow from the earth and for it to receive the autumn and spring rains. You, too, must be patient (James 5:7-8 NCV)

Patience begins with a *choice* for patience before the *need* for patience occurs. Since sandpaper people are forever with us, the question is not how to eliminate the difficult relationships in life, but how we can patiently respond to the people who rub us the wrong way.

Patience Chooses a Better Perspective

Patient people are people who have grown and matured—and as they have grown, so has their perspective. Several years ago, my family and I visited the small Texas town where I grew up and attended college. I wanted my children to see just how good they have it now, compared to my childhood. As a scholarship student majoring in music, I was required to participate in every musical production on campus. Jered and Danna quizzed me, and memories spilled out of the past as I told story after story of my first performance, a severe case of stage fright, and the long tedious rehearsals. I described the intimidating stage and the ridiculous antics we pulled while waiting in the wings to go on, wondering how many thousands of people were in the audience.

Both Jered and Danna seemed duly impressed, until we pulled up in front of the music building. It was so small! When I stepped out on that strangely unfamiliar stage, I thought, *There has to be a mistake. The stage where I performed years ago was much bigger!* It wasn't. My perspective had simply been altered by the years. As we grow and mature, our understanding and perspective of life should grow and mature as well, allowing us to see things in a different light. That light of understanding must then be focused on our sandpaper people, enabling us to grow in patience and cultivate a new perspective of their presence and purpose in our lives.

> Saul's soldiers thought Goliath was too big to kill. David thought he was too big to miss! The victory came because of a different perspective!

Impatience is the automatic response of immaturity, as the apostle Paul indicates in 1 Corinthians 13:11: "When I was a child, I spoke and thought and reasoned as a child does" (NLT). God uses trials to wean us from seeing and responding to circumstances and relationships in a childish way. Patient people have learned to focus on the solution—not the problem. Saul's soldiers thought Goliath was too big to kill. David thought he was too big to miss! The victory came because of a different perspective! God ordains and monitors difficult relationships, using them to cultivate patience and understanding where there was once only impatience and an immature reaction to those flesh-and-blood tools of refinement known as sandpaper people. "Patient people have great understanding" (Proverbs 14:29 NCV).

Patience Learns to Laugh More

The book of Proverbs is rich with the benefits of joy and laughter. "A relaxed attitude lengthens life" (14:30 TLB). "A cheerful heart has a continual feast" (15:15). We need to approach the difficult relationships in life with joy and laughter. When it comes to dealing with sandpaper people, our watchword should be "Lighten up." A sense of humor encourages patience, and patience always thrives in a joy-filled heart.

I have little or no patience with road hogs and seem to find ample opportunities for expressing my less-than-favorable opinion of the way they drive. We live in a small but rapidly growing town just outside of Charlotte, North Carolina. Because the town has outgrown its winding country roads, traffic from the city into our community is a daily nightmare. At one particular spot, a double lane narrows to a single lane. The change is clearly marked by several strategically placed signs and most people—the nice velvet people—pull into the single left lane long before the road narrows, knowing the right lane will soon merge with the left lane.

The sandpaper people, on the other hand, spot the merging lane signs and consider them an open invitation to speed ahead, worming their way into the long line of waiting cars. I consider it my personal responsibility to educate these road hogs in "The Ins and Outs of Traffic Courtesy According to Mary," by refusing to let them barge in front of me and secure a spot in "my" line. I never make eye contact with these sandpaper drivers, thus denying their existence while inching along as close as possible to the car in front of me, determined to hold my ground.

One day, however, I met my match. I saw him coming but stood firm in my resolve to enforce my "don't let 'em in no matter what" rule. Time after time, he tried unsuccessfully to pull in front of me. I ignored him. He honked. I feigned deafness. Finally, in one last-ditch effort to merge before his lane disappeared, the man rolled down his window and yelled, "Look!" I couldn't help myself. He was holding up a napkin that read "Pleeeeeeease!" I burst out laughing and motioned for him to pull in front of me. He applauded and danced a seated jig in celebration of his hard-earned place in line.

Life is like that—sandpaper people trying to capture your attention, ignoring the signs, breaking the rules while barging into your life. It takes a sense of humor to navigate the tumultuous waters of difficult relationships without capsizing. The secret of joy-filled relationships is to count on God's strength instead of our own. Joy comes from a continual reliance upon Him to hammer down the relationship mountains before us, making the path straight and pointing it in the right direction. Paul said it well— "I have learned the secret of being content in any and every situation, whether well fed or hungry, whether living in plenty or in want. I can do everything through him who gives me strength" (Philippians 4:12-13). This passage could easily read, "I have learned the secret of being content in any and every *relationship* by depending upon the power of God's love at work. I can *love anyone* through him who gives me strength." As we learn to laugh more and cultivate our God-given sense of humor, patience and the ability to deal with the difficult relationships in life will flourish.

Patience Chooses to Love More

In what is commonly known as the "love chapter" of the Bible, Paul writes the profoundly correlating phrases, "Love is patient, love is kind" (1 Corinthians 13:4). Sandpaper people need to be loved but wrongly believe that in order to experience love they must first be *lovable*. The opposite is true, and it's foreign to the way a sandpaper person thinks. We must first be *loved* in order to be lovable. Because of this faulty pattern of thinking, sandpaper people will demand love instead of accepting it. Their abrasive behavior, a desperate attempt to hold emotional hostages until the ransom of love is paid, drives away the very ones who would give them the love they seek. We grow impatient with their futility. But in God's eyes, impatience is a love problem.

A heart filled with love refuses to entertain irritations, not even those caused by the abrasive behavior of sandpaper people. However, a heart filled with anger is a magnet for irritations, especially the abrasive behavior of sandpaper people. "Be humble and gentle. Be patient with each other, making allowance for each other's faults because of your love" (Ephesians 4:2 NLT). "Making allowance for each other's faults" means we are to handle relationships in a way that anticipates their inevitable faults.

When our children became teenagers, Dan and I realized a new plan for their allowances was needed. We were tired of being asked for money by two kids who enjoyed the privilege of an allowance. There seemed to be confusion about what their allowances should cover as opposed to those expenses that would fall under the responsibility of parental funding. For example, our son would fill his truck with gas and then drive my car. Our daughter would buy a new pair of shoes and then need money for a movie, since she had spent her "very own money" for shoes, clearly a "parent purchase" item. Even though Jered and Danna seemed content with the existing plan, we weren't. Dan and I sat down with each child to formulate a clear strategy for spending. Confusion and frustration then disappeared because the right plan was in place.

God's right plan for dealing with sandpaper people includes an "emotional allowance"—setting aside part of our emotional energy to cover their faults and allow for their weaknesses. In other words, we are supposed to "admonish the unruly, encourage the fainthearted, help the weak and be patient with all men" (1 Thessalonians 5:14 NASB). Sandpaper people are unruly—frequently careless or out of line in their behavior. The word "unruly" applies to soldiers who refuse to follow orders, insisting on doing things their own way. Sound familiar? It is the watchword of every card-carrying sandpaper person. Patience lovingly corrects and points out the right way.

Sandpaper people tend to give up easily, feeding the failure that has become a familiar companion, training their feeble hearts to despair while persuading their fragile spirits to quit. Patience comforts these hard-to-love people, refusing to give up on them when everyone else has walked away. The "weak" ones are those who are weak in their faith—the baby Christians. New believers awkwardly stumble through their first steps into the world of Christianity and are often perceived to be "rough around the edges." Patience not only reassures these frightened little lambs that they belong, but also offers to walk with them until they grow stronger and their path is sure.

His name was Sam. I fell in love with him the first time I saw him. I was standing at the door of my second-grade classroom, anxiously waiting to greet the 30 students who had been assigned to me for the school year. Though Sam was smaller than the other children, he walked with the earned confidence of one who had seen more than he should have seen at such a young age. What he lacked in size, he more than made up for in personality and attitude. He was a blatant flirt, and I was a goner as soon as he gazed up at me with strikingly blue eyes that caught my heart. His flashing two cavernous dimples completed its capture.

I will never forget the pain in his words, though. "My name is Sam. I am dumb and stupid and I can't do nothin' right. I get mad real easy and break things. I just thought you oughta know." It took only a few minutes for Sam to begin what I suspected was his usual attempt to prove those words true. He swept through the quickly filling classroom, destruction in his hands. Papers were ripped and tossed aside. Children shrank away in fear from his now scowling face. When a little girl laughed, Sam thought she was laughing at him and knocked her to the floor. I had seen enough. Taking him by the arm, I marched him out of the classroom and down the hall. He wasn't surprised or particularly concerned. It was all very familiar to him; but what came next wasn't.

Looking for a place to sit, I stopped in front of a bench and, much to my own surprise, instinctively pulled this precious little man into my arms with a fierce hug. "Sam, it's wrong to tell a lie," I whispered. Stunned, he drew back. "What do you mean? I didn't tell no lie." Cupping his freckled face in my hands, I whispered, "Yes, you did. You said you were dumb and stupid and couldn't do anything right. That is a lie. I don't know who told you that and I don't care. It's not true—is it, Sam?" His eyes filled with tears—and a tiny ray of hope appeared. It was enough. Slowly, Sam shook his head, a damp smile creeping across his now softening face. "Nope. I reckon it ain't if you say so." I smiled back, "Well, I say so. Now why don't you be my assistant today and help me pass out papers?" Together, we walked back to the classroom and to a new beginning for one little sandpaper person.

That year I taught Sam and he taught me. I'm not certain who learned the most but this I do know—the more we love, the more patience we will have; and the more patience we have, the more we will love. I often wonder just how many "Sams" are waiting for someone—anyone—who will choose to unleash the power of patience and by doing so, unleash the power of love as well.

SANDPAPER FOLIAGE

The sandpaper plant is a bushy tree with rough, sandpapery leaves. The ¾-inch furry fruit are dark when ripe, and they appear on the trunk and larger branches. The tree is often associated with creek banks, has a rough stem used to smooth the surface of crafts, and produces beautiful flowers that are "fluffy" in appearance. The fruit are edible raw when fully ripe, but the furry skin can be an irritant and must be peeled off before eating.

Sandpaper vine:

Common name:	Queen's Wreath, Purple Wreath, Sandpaper Vine
Scientific names:	*Petrea volubilis; Petrea kohautiana*
Family:	Verbenaceae
Frost tolerance:	Semitender in Phoenix, established plants suffer below 26° F
Sun exposure:	Full sun or light shade
Origin:	Central America
Growth habits:	Vine to 40 feet long or self-supporting shrub; bluish calices remain after the plant's flowers are gone
Watering needs:	Keep moist until the plant is established, regular water thereafter
Propagation:	Layering, or semi-hardwood cuttings with bottom heat[5]

Six

Be Forgiving:
Forgive and Forget

Be kind to one another, tenderhearted,
forgiving one another,
even as God in Christ forgave you.
Ephesians 4:32 NKJV

ONE WEEKEND I TAUGHT WITH DAN for the five worship services of our rapidly growing church. I was very comfortable standing before hundreds and even thousands of women, but to teach a congregation filled with both men and women was something new and a bit unsettling. After the final service I breathed a sigh of relief, feeling good about the truths I had shared and people's response to those truths. In fact, I honestly thought it had gone well. Church members were kind, while the pastoral staff directed a steady stream of encouragement my way. It had been a busy week of juggling family responsibilities with study time. I was exhausted, emotionally drained, and definitely *not* in the mood to cook. So we headed to the nearest restaurant to meet the other pastors and their wives for lunch.

During each worship service, ushers passed out comment cards for those attending to share prayer needs or concerns. Each week, the cards were collected and given to Dan on Monday morning. However, on this particular Sunday, a new volunteer, unaware of the protocol concerning the cards but enthusiastic about his first place of service, handed the large stack of cards to me and asked, "Can you give these to Pastor Dan?" I didn't have the heart to correct him. "I would be glad to," I said. Smiling, the volunteer thanked me for allowing him to serve and walked away, whistling. *Now that's what it's all about. I love these people,* I thought. It would be quite some time before those words would again ring true in my spirit.

Before we even made it out of the church parking lot, I began to read through the thick stack of cards, curious about the comments. I must admit I secretly longed for words of praise and affirmation. But I was stunned by words of indictment aimed straight at me. "Has this church gotten so liberal that we now allow women preachers to stand in God's pulpit?" The words found their mark. The card had no signature, of course, but it could easily have been signed, "Your Loyal Sandpaper Person." Dan took one look at my face and said, "Honey, what's wrong?" I handed him the card, tears streaming down my cheeks. Furious at the nameless enemy, Dan wiped away my tears and, in an effort to lessen the blow, vowed to hunt down the person and take him out. It sounded like a great plan to me! My heart, wounded and bleeding from the piercing words, slowly began to harden in an attempt to numb the pain. Sandpaper people often have that effect on the heart.

As we pulled into the restaurant parking lot, our youth pastor, Garland Robertson, and his wife, Kelly, pulled into the parking space beside us. Kelly took one look at me and asked, "Mary, what's wrong?" I promptly fell apart, handing her the card. Anger flashed in her eyes as she thrust the harsh words into the massive hands of her husband, a gentle giant of a man who has always been fiercely protective of me. After reading it, he pulled me into one of his famous bear hugs and said, "Don't let one ignorant critic ruin what God did this weekend."

I tried to put the hurtful comment behind me and honestly thought I had—until one Tuesday morning when, for the first time in weeks, I sensed His presence. I was preparing for my weekly Bible study, wondering what in the world I could possibly offer any woman attending when all I felt was emptiness and the barrenness of a spiritual wasteland. Standing at the bathroom sink, I prayed one more time for God to show me the reason behind my desert experience. God whispered to my heart, *Mary, you haven't forgiven him.* I knew exactly who He meant, but I wasn't quite ready to release my anger. God persisted. *And since that day, you haven't forgiven anyone else who has hurt you.* Caught off guard by the revelation, I knew it was true. I had collected every hurt and criticism since reading that comment card, as if building a case of revenge that would be tried in the court of my own pain. In fact, I had collected so many hurts and done such a good job of stashing them away that they had built a wall between my joy and my heart.

As this fresh revelation washed over me, Danna came running into the room to show me her newest Lego creation. Reaching the bathroom doorway, she tripped and fell, her plastic house crashing to the floor, and shattering into hundreds of pieces. The silence was deafening as we stared at hours of work—all gone. I couldn't speak, but the words of my daughter came straight from the heart of God. "Does it matter, Mama?" In that moment, I saw myself running to the Father with my collection of hurts, spilling them at His feet. I had invested a great deal of time and effort amassing those hurts, tucking them away until an enormous wall of wounded pain was formed, blocking the flow of His joy and the light of His presence. The wall that only moments ago had seemed irremovable was effortlessly ripped apart by His words of love. *Mary,* He said, *they don't matter! Forgive each one. Lay them down. Let them go. They don't really matter.* Over the next few weeks, I worked through my anger and hurt to freedom and light. I was set free.

The Antidote to Failure

Sandpaper people are hard to forgive—but they are the very ones who need forgiveness the most and most often. Many times, the sandpaper merely covers a wound that has never healed, a wrong that has never been forgiven, or a hideous sin that has never been confronted and confessed. It is paradoxical that sandpaper people orchestrate difficult circumstances and broken relationships in an unconscious attempt to prove they don't deserve and shouldn't dare expect forgiveness. In other words, they will deliberately set themselves up to fail. That's where forgiveness comes in.

When sandpaper people experience forgiveness, their plan of self-destruction is thwarted. Guilt and blame feed the hellish insecurity lodged in the hearts and minds of sandpaper people, determining their coarse actions, dictating their grating words and opinions while corroding their relationships—until someone chooses to see that difficult person through the eyes of God. Until someone chooses to forgive them, sandpaper and all. In the Bible, we find the story of such a man, a king who chose to forgive the unforgivable.

> The kingdom of heaven may be compared to a certain king who wished to settle accounts with his slaves. And when he had begun to settle them, there was brought to him one who owed him ten thousand talents. But since he did not have the means to repay, his lord commanded him to be sold, along with his wife and children and all that he had, and repayment to be made. The slave therefore falling down, prostrated himself before him, saying, "Have patience with me, and I will repay you everything." And the lord of that slave felt compassion and released him and forgave him the debt. But that slave went out and found one of his fellow slaves who owed him a hundred denarii;

and he seized him and began to choke him, saying, "Pay back what you owe." So his fellow slave fell down and began to entreat him, saying, "Have patience with me and I will repay you." He was unwilling however, but went and threw him in prison until he should pay back what was owed. So when his fellow slaves saw what had happened, they were deeply grieved and came and reported to their lord all that had happened. Then summoning him, his lord said to him, "You wicked slave, I forgave you all that debt because you entreated me. Should you not also have had mercy on your fellow slave, even as I had mercy on you?" And his lord, moved with anger, handed him over to the torturers until he should repay all that was owed him (Mathew 18:23-34 NASB).

Even kings have sandpaper people. The slave in this story definitely fits the bill of someone who is difficult to deal with and almost impossible to forgive. Still, the king rightly chose to forgive him, even when he abused the forgiveness granted him by the king. The slave didn't understand that, once forgiven, we must then forgive. Perhaps the slave, like so many sandpaper people, didn't fully understand what forgiveness really is.

Forgiveness is neither justifying why a person acted the way they did nor forgetting about the wrong done. Forgiveness is more than asking God to forgive that person or asking God to forgive our anger toward them. Denying the existence of emotional pain is not part of true forgiveness. Forgiveness is the act of setting someone free from an obligation to you that results from a wrong done to you. But forgiveness is the cancellation of a debt. Forgiveness does not hinge on anything the one in debt does or doesn't do. When a debt is cancelled, it is sent away, never to be revisited or reclaimed.

An Immense Need

Because sandpaper people often unknowingly inflict pain, they rarely ask to be forgiven. But forgiveness doesn't wait on an invitation. It simply works. Forgiveness is a demonstration of love that leads first to action and then to an attitude. True forgiveness is a powerful weapon in the war against emotional pain and a key part of every relationship—especially those relationships with sandpaper people. In fact, I suspect that many sandpaper people exist to teach us to forgive the way God forgives.

Once we understand the true meaning of forgiveness, we will recognize the enormous need for forgiveness in every life and every relationship. The book of Mark offers a glimpse of the role forgiveness plays in a life of victory. "When you are praying, first forgive anyone you are holding a grudge against, so that your Father in heaven will forgive you your sins too" (11:25 NLT) When we refuse to forgive others, we are blocking the flow of forgiveness to our own life. The best reason to forgive is simply because God says so. He isn't impressed with our knowledge of forgiveness; he is impressed when we practice forgiveness. I really believe sandpaper people are deeply impacted by freely offered forgiveness. We are naturally expected to love those who are easy to love. Anyone can do that. But to love those who are unlovable, to forgive those who are unforgivable, is beyond the measure and scope of human understanding.

> He has brought in His remodeling crew as often as needed, demolishing the old me and building a new one.

Forgiveness is part of God's character, and as fully devoted followers of Jesus Christ, we need to look just like our Father when it comes to practicing forgiveness. The apostle Paul writes, "Be kind to one another, tenderhearted, forgiving one another, even as God in Christ forgave you" (Ephesians 4:32 NKJV). Part of the proof of being a Christian is giving others what God has given to us. How much mercy do you need? How much forgiveness do you require? That is how much you must forgive.

Forgiveness is a gift we give ourselves. The warning of Hebrews 12:14-15 is one we need to heed, especially when dealing with sandpaper people. "Try to stay out of all quarrels, and seek to live a clean and holy life, for one who is not holy will not see the Lord. Look after each other so that not one of you will fail to find God's best blessings. Watch out that no bitterness takes root among you, for as it springs up it causes deep trouble, hurting many in their spiritual lives" (NCV). When we refuse to forgive someone, we make them our jailer. The minute I start hating someone, the minute I withhold forgiveness, I become that person's slave! Justice and revenge belong solely in the hands of God. "Do not take revenge, my friends, but leave room for God's wrath, for it is written: 'It is mine to avenge; I will repay,' says the Lord" (Romans 12:19).

Forgiveness is our best opportunity to change a sandpaper person. "Now it is time to forgive him and comfort him. Otherwise, he may become so bitter and discouraged that he won't be able to recover." Sandpaper people are covered with layers of the bitterness they create in the lives of those who cannot or will not forgive them. Discouragement sets in, and the possibility of changing seems unattainable. That discouragement leads to resentment and results in angry behavior, the kind of behavior we experience at the hand of sandpaper people. Forgiveness breaks this vicious cycle of despair and defeat by stripping away the bitterness, gutting the discouragement, and replacing it with unconditional love.

I promised myself I would never remodel a house, but there we were—buying a townhouse that needed so much work even the realtor couldn't believe we wanted it. Why didn't someone stop me? In my ignorance I pressed on, the sale was made, and we went to work. Actually, my son and husband went to work while I went crazy! I had no idea how horrible the process of remodeling could be.

Layers of dirt, grime, stains, and ugliness were stripped away. Rotten kitchen cabinets were torn from the walls while old, rusty appliances were hauled away to be replaced by shiny, new ones. We pretty much gutted the entire place and rebuilt it—while living in it. I will never forget the day I woke up to see a toilet sitting at the foot of our bed. Where does it say that I have to live with a toilet sitting at the foot of my bed? It was at that moment I resolved never to set foot in another "fixer-upper."

I am so thankful God doesn't feel the same way about me. He has brought in His remodeling crew as often as needed, demolishing the old me and building a new one. He did a huge renovation on me through a two-year battle with clinical depression. While sitting at the bottom of a dark and slimy pit, the Father lovingly stripped away old fears and insecurities. From the walls of my heart, He tore the rotten attitudes, undisciplined thoughts, and unholy desires that had deceptively walked me to the edge of my pit—then triumphantly pushed me in. But new dreams replaced old, rusty ones. God pretty much gutted my old life to build a new one, a better one, and a stronger one.

God delights in transforming sandpaper people into velvet people. We become part of that transformation process when we love and forgive sandpaper people. Forgiveness proves the power of His love and sets that power free to work. The Gospel of John underscores the truth that the heart of every faithful disciple beats with God's supernatural love and forgiveness. "Your love for one another will prove to the world that you are my disciples" (13:35 NLT). What draws the attention of the world to us as believers is not that we don't fight or argue, and certainly not that we never disagree or hurt each other. What draws the world's attention is how we forgive each other—especially when that forgiveness is given to difficult people, sandpaper people, people who rub us the wrong way. And in order to forgive, we must know the steps of obedience that forgiveness requires.

STEP 1: TAKE THE INITIATIVE

A heart of forgiveness is willing to take the first step toward reconciliation, even when the person in need of forgiveness is annoying, abrasive, and irritating. Notice Matthew 18:23: "The king wanted to bring his accounts up to date" (NASB). I am certain the king was aware that his slave was not one of the most likable or popular slaves in town. After all, he was up to his eyeballs in debt and had made no effort to repay it. If the slave was willing to steal from the king, he was willing to steal from anyone.

The slave not only lacked integrity but was also prone to violent behavior and seemed incapable of controlling his emotions. He choked the man who owed him money instead of handling the debt in the same way the king handled his. The fact that his fellow slaves were so quick to tell the king about his behavior makes me think he was not well-liked. In my opinion, the slave was a sandpaper person. Still, the king took the initiative in making things right between himself and the slave. The slave's abuse of the king's forgiveness resulted in the slave's imprisonment.

The same is true in our lives today. When we allow conflict to remain unresolved, we will eventually find ourselves held hostage, imprisoned by our own disobedience. The king understood this truth. He didn't initiate the forgiveness process because the slave deserved forgiveness, recognized his need of forgiveness, or even asked for forgiveness. The king took the first step because it was the right thing to do and because he understood the power of forgiveness as well as the concept of submission to a higher authority. He was the king, accustomed to having his orders obeyed without question. I imagine he rewarded those under his leadership who did what he asked. The king was a wise man who understood the value of keeping his accounts settled.

We need to live with that same attitude—determined to keep our relationship accounts settled and up to date. Allowing hurts to accumulate will always result in a bitter spirit and a heart bent on revenge. Revenge always results in destruction of some kind. I heard about a truck driver who dropped in at an all-night restaurant in Broken Bow, Nebraska. The waitress had just served him, when three leather-jacketed motorcyclists walked in and began antagonizing him, apparently looking for a fight. One of them grabbed the hamburger off his plate. Another took a handful of his French fries, and the third drank his coffee. The trucker seemed unfazed by their maliciousness and calmly picked up his check, walked to the cash register, paid for his meal, and without even a backward glance, went out the door. The waitress watched him drive away. When she returned, one of the cyclists laughingly said, "Well, he's not much of a man, is he?" She replied, "I don't know about that, but he's sure not much of a truck driver. He just ran over three motorcycles out in the parking lot."

When we allow offenses to accumulate, the consequences are ours to bear. Forgiveness requires an ongoing commitment on our part to be right with each other, whatever it takes, for as long as it takes—a radical attitude that includes a chosen willingness to take the first step, just as Jesus did. "God showed his great love for us by sending Christ to die for us while we were still sinners," Paul writes in Romans 5:8 (NLT). Jesus Christ, the perfect Son of God, did not wait until we shaped up, repented, changed our ways, or got our act together. He came. He took the first step. We must accept our part of the responsibility in the hurt and quit waiting for anyone to change. When it comes to forgiveness, we are to turn our back on revenge and take the first step toward reconciliation.

STEP 2: FORGIVE YOURSELF

Because sandpaper people cannot forgive themselves, they find it hard to believe that anyone else can forgive them. But forgiveness is a gift. We can't earn it. We can never be good enough to deserve it, nor can we buy it. All we can do is accept it. What a great promise we find in John 1:9: "If we confess our sins, He is faithful and just to forgive us our sins and to cleanse us from every wrong" (NLT). In order to forgive, we must recognize and accept the fact we are forgiven. Until then, we will live a "payback" lifestyle, operating from guilt instead of grace.

Suppose a man buys a new car but continues to walk everywhere. Neighbors comment on the beautiful car sitting in his driveway. Every Saturday, he spends hours washing and waxing it, and in his spare time he reads and studies the owner's manual. Sure, the man owns the car—but he's missing the *joy* of owning it. The same is true for Christians who neither accept nor practice forgiveness. Day after day, we struggle to rise above the weight of our sin, living seemingly impotent lives lacking freedom and peace. If that is the case, what we are really saying is that God's love is insufficient—that the forgiveness Jesus bought with His death on the cross was not enough to pay for our sin. An absurd way of thinking, isn't it? Our refusal to accept, walk in, and offer forgiveness is just as absurd. Right now, choose to forgive yourself and walk in the freedom of a clean heart before God.

STEP 3: FORGIVE THE DEBT

Do you remember the last words of Jesus on the cross? "It is finished!" The most literal translation would be "Paid in full!" Have you ever paid off a loan? I will never forget paying off my first car loan. After sending in my forty-eighth and final payment, I celebrated the fact that I was finally the very proud, bumper-to-bumper owner of my bright blue and ever-so-compact Chevrolet Vega. There were those who said you couldn't drive my car—you had to wear it. Others described the bright color as "strangely unique." But to me it was the most beautiful car in the world because it was mine, all mine. I quickly found other places to spend the money once allocated to the car payment and went on with life—until I opened my mailbox to find the loan papers. Stamped in bold, red letters across the document were the words "Paid in Full." I danced all the way into the house!

Part of forgiveness is releasing the person from the debt we think is owed to us. In Matthew 18:27, we see that the king "forgave the debt and let him go." As a leader, the king seemed to understand that sometimes the best thing to do is to let something go and cut your losses instead of allowing the weight of an unpaid debt to deplete your mental and emotional energy.

Several years ago we decided it was time to sell one of our old, junky cars. We had several from which to choose, but this particular vehicle needed a lot of work and even more prayer. We lovingly called it our "fishing car" because when it rained, leaks formed a puddle in the trunk, furnishing a dandy little fishing hole. In the right hands, the fishing car could last several more years. A man who worked for our church agreed to buy it. He and Dan worked out the terms. He was to pay a certain amount each month until the car was paid for. No papers were signed because, after all, it was a business agreement between two ministers.

Well, some lessons are learned the hard way. Dan gave the man the title and the car keys. He gave us nothing. Not one penny. My husband talked with him several times. The man always responded with the promise that he would make a payment "soon." "Soon" never came. I was furious, not so much because of the money—although it would have come in handy—but because this sandpaper man was taking advantage of my husband's giving heart and ticking me off in the process. I ranted and fumed for weeks until Dan said, "Honey, I have decided to forgive the debt on that old car." Well, I decided *not* to, and my anger grew into full-blown resentment and bitterness.

A few months later, the man quit his job at the church and went to work for a nearby grocery store—*my* grocery store. I soon learned that God has a sense of humor, because almost every time I went to the store, the car thief, as I called him, was there. Every time I saw him, anger consumed my heart. I finally realized that this car situation was robbing my whole life of joy. So one day I decided to give him the car—it was the only thing I could do to experience peace.

In my mind, I created a scene of driving to the grocery store, handing him the car keys, and saying, "Merry Christmas! Enjoy your new car." It wasn't Christmas, and the car was far from new, but it worked. I forgave the debt in my heart and let it go. And the most amazing thing happened. *I* was the one who was set free. From that day on, every time I saw the man I waved and smiled. He began avoiding me, unable to look me in the eye. Remember, I told you that God has a sense of humor? A few months later I saw the man driving a different car. I soon learned from one of his co-workers that "his old car just up and died." Enough said.

Forgiving the debt is a deliberate choice made by an act of your will. You may not feel forgiving. It doesn't matter. Just do it, and many times the feelings will follow that choice—though other times they won't. Feelings are irrelevant, but obedience is imperative. Don't base the validity of what you are doing on how you feel. Make the choice to forgive and then obey. Someone once said, "We put our resentments in cold storage and then pull the switch to let them thaw out again. Our grudges are taken out to the lake of prayer to drown them and we end up giving them a swimming lesson. How often have we torn up the canceled note but hung on to the wastebasket holding the pieces? This is not to say that human forgiveness doesn't occur; only that it is rare and that much that passes for forgiveness is often not so at all." God calls us to forgive the debt.

STEP 4: PRACTICE ACCEPTANCE

Forgiveness requires acceptance without a demand for change. We cannot make others responsible for meeting our needs, acting a certain way, rising to our standards, or fulfilling our expectations. If we are brutally honest with ourselves, we will recognize the not-so-lovely truth that what we really want from the sandpaper people in our lives is for them to become a carbon copy of...us! However, one of the most valuable lessons we can learn from sandpaper people is that "all things work together for good" (Romans 8:28). "All" really does mean *all*. Every relationship comes into our life for a purpose. Some come to replenish us, while others come to remake us, relentlessly abrading the rough edges that don't fit the eternally molded shape of who we are in Christ. God sometimes allows difficult relationships to drive us to our knees, on our face before Him—and anything or anyone who makes us cry out to God can be counted as a blessing.

Several years ago, a blessing came into my life in the form of a woman who, from the first time we met, decided I was a complete phony and hypocrite. She then proceeded to tell me so through icy stares and sarcastic comments and by avoiding my presence whenever possible. Over the next two years, she twisted the meaning of every word I said, misinterpreted my every action, and found everything I did offensive. Finally I confronted her, but it only made things worse—until I chose to forgive her in spite of it all.

As the months went by, I gained new insight into her life and began to understand the sources of her anger—the loss of her ministry dream, a disabled son, and financial strain. I examined my own heart, asking myself some tough questions. *What am I doing that would give her a wrong impression? How would it feel to be so misunderstood?* While the whole circumstance was very painful, it was also one of great growth. Today, because of my experience with this sandpaper person, I now sift through any criticism for even a nugget of truth. It is a good thing.

STEP 5: PURSUE RECONCILIATION

Reconciliation is often an ignored step in the process of forgiveness. I think the reason is that reconciliation is tough, demanding that we surrender our will and crucify self. Nevertheless, Matthew 5:23 clearly outlines the importance of forgiveness that leads to restoration and reconciliation: "If you are standing before the altar in the Temple, offering a sacrifice to God, and suddenly remember that a friend has something against you, leave your sacrifice there beside the altar and go and apologize and be reconciled to him, and then come and offer your sacrifice to God" (NLT). I wonder just how many gifts laid on the altar are deemed unacceptable by God because they are given from an unforgiving heart. How many offerings are pronounced useless because the giver is unwilling to forgive? Reconciliation comes when forgiveness is complete.

The method of reconciliation will be different for every situation, but reconciliation needs to be proportionate to and as far-reaching as the hurt. A carefully penned note may suffice. A timely phone call or a face-to-face meeting may be the solution.

In my experience, when my heart is genuinely committed to forgiving someone, I know exactly what to do in order for reconciliation to take place in that relationship. My heart knows when forgiveness is complete. God is the One who heals the wound, but forgiveness puts us in the correct posture for Him to do so.

When we daily practice forgiveness, it is stored in our hearts and lives so that when the hardest moments of hurt come, it is easier to forgive. In other words, we can develop the habit of forgiving.

The king's slave was forgiven, but he refused to forgive others. Prison was his reward. The king had every right to demand full and immediate payment from the ungrateful slave, but he chose forgiveness instead. Freedom was the treasure the king won. When it comes to dealing with sandpaper people, forgiveness pleases God, and it frees us to forgive and to be forgiven.

SANDPAPER FROG

The sandpaper frog was given its name because of the male's rough, sandpapery skin when in breeding condition. Also known as Fletcher's frog (after an Australian zoologist), this frog lives in moist forests. It is usually found close to pools and streams but is rarely seen except in the summer breeding season. The purring call of courting males is quite distinctive. It lasts about a second and sounds like "gar-r-r-up." The tadpoles of this species are cannibalistic, with the weaker, smaller ones becoming prey for their larger siblings. This frog also produces a powerful skin toxin.[6]

Seven

Be Caring:
Meet a Need

*If your enemy is hungry, give him food to eat;
if he is thirsty, give him water to drink.
In doing this, you will heap burning coals on his head,
and the Lord will reward you.*

Proverbs 25:21-22

THE MORE I WORK AND INTERACT with sandpaper people, the more I realize there is always a reason for their abrasive behavior. That sandpaper may very well be a well-chosen mask, a creatively crafted defense, a tediously built wall, or a bandage carefully applied to some deeply hidden wound that has never fully healed. Watching abrasive people is like watching a child who has picked a battle and come out fighting, daring someone to love him.

We once lived in a South Florida neighborhood filled with older couples. The housing was less expensive, the noise level was lower, and our children were quickly adopted by several sets of grandparents who seemed committed to thoroughly spoiling them. Although most of our neighbors soon became friends, one elderly couple made our list of people to avoid because they complained about everything. Our dog barked too much, our kids were too loud, our garbage can was in the wrong place…you name it, they didn't like it. Our very existence seemed to be an irritation to these grouches. (I am certain they considered us their very own sandpaper family.) They were definitely *not* my favorite neighbors, a fact that was heightened by the approaching holidays.

I love Christmas and everything associated with it, especially the chance to focus on the birth of a baby who came to earth, born here because of a love that reaches everyone, including sandpaper people. With only days left until Christmas Day, my children and I were busy with holiday preparations, wrapping gifts, baking cookies, decorating the house, and making Christmas cards. We sent the usual generic, store-bought cards to most people on our list, but reserved those made by my children for the "extra special" people in our lives.

It was unusual weather for Hollywood, a chilly day—the faithful South Florida sun strangely shrouded in dark clouds, a light mist falling. I sensed the children growing restless as the rain persisted and decided to head trouble off at the pass by announcing that today was "Make Christmas Cards for our Neighbors Day." My job was to locate our collection of traditional Christmas carols, slice and bake my famous "must have at all holidays" sugar cookies, then mix hot chocolate in our favorite Christmas mugs while Jered and Danna scampered away to invade the toy closet and the craft box to gather the necessary supplies for our project.

It was a perfect day, a veritable Kodak-moment-filled day— until my son looked up from his brightly colored card to ask, "Mama, what kind of card are we going to make for them?" A small, unwelcome knot began to form in my stomach as dread snaked its way around my heart. I knew exactly what he was asking but hoped I was dead wrong. "Who are you talking about, son?" I asked innocently (well, not so innocently). "The Smiths, Mom. What kind of card are we going to make for the Smiths?" my sweethearted but determined child persisted. I never should have asked.

Memories of terse phone calls and sarcastic notes left on the front porch and back fence tumbled into my heart, pushing aside any semblance of the Christmas spirit. Scathing words poured from my angry heart, "Son, why would you want to make a Christmas card for the Smiths, when they are so mean to us? They don't like our dog, our garbage can, or anyone in our family, as far as I can tell. They obviously want nothing to do with us. And besides, they don't even celebrate Christmas." In that moment, the tables were turned. I was the pupil and my young son became the teacher, patiently explaining the rules according to God—not Mom: "Because I don't think they really mean all of that stuff, Mom. I think they are just old people nobody loves. I mean, I never see any cars at their house, and they're always at home. No kids live there. Do you know they don't even have a cat or dog? Can you believe that, Mom? Maybe they're just sad and lonely. Don't you think we should do something about it?"

Staring into the compassion-filled eyes of my forgiving son, I knew what we had to do. We made two magnificent cards! The oven timer buzzed, reminding me that the sugar cookies were done. Danna piped up with "Cookies, Mama. Let's take cookies!" I was obviously outnumbered. Rummaging through the box of Christmas dishes waiting to be unpacked, I uncovered a brightly colored Christmas tin and, holding it in the air, watched my fresh-from-God children break out in applause and cheers. It was a winner!

When the cards were finished, the sticky, glittery envelopes sealed, and the still-warm sugar cookies carefully packed, I actually heard myself utter words I never thought I would say: "It's time to visit the Smiths." What in the world was I thinking? What had I done? "Wait, Mom!" Jered shouted. After whispering something to Danna, both kids raced to their rooms. In seconds, they came rushing out with two of their favorite books in each hand. I was clueless at this point. Seeing the confusion on my face, Jered patiently explained, "Maybe they would like to read us a story, Mom." I had serious doubts but thought, at this point, anything was worth a try. After all, we were already in over our heads. What did a few more feet matter?

Who Is My Neighbor?

Diving into new winter coats, we headed out the front door to what I desperately hoped would not be a complete disaster. I prayed every step of the way, asking God to either work a miracle or let the gruff old couple be gone. I secretly hoped for a "drop and run" mission. When we reached the Smith's sidewalk, I made one last-ditch effort to avoid the inevitable. "What a shame. There's no car. I guess they aren't home. We'll try later," I said. (Later—as in 20 years or so.) My children were not to be trifled with. They stood their ground, glaring at me. "Fine, we'll ring the doorbell." I said. Taking a deep breath, I voiced one last silent but hopeful prayer and pushed the button. No answer. Awesome! "Well, let's just leave the goodies and try again when your daddy's home and can come with us," I cheerfully suggested.

Weak with relief, I turned to make my escape, reluctant children in tow, when the front door creaked open and Mr. Smith barked, "What are you selling? Whatever it is, we don't want any!" That did it! I can handle someone being mean to me, but being mean to my kids is an entirely different matter. I had just about reached my limit with these people and was more than ready to tell the scowling man what I thought of his attitude. But before I could get out even one of my many angry words, Danna shyly handed him the card she had made and with the pride of an artist, proudly said, "I made this for you and your mother." Great! Just great! Things were definitely looking up! Danna had just doubled the age of the grumpy old woman by calling Mrs. Smith the mother of the grumpy old man. "I have one, too!" chimed Jered. I held my breath, expecting an explosion at any moment and wondering how in the world I was going to finish my Christmas shopping from a jail cell. The next sound I heard was unbelievable. It was a laugh. A laugh? I could not believe my ears, but sure enough, our sandpaper neighbor was laughing. I had never even seen the man smile!

Opening the screen door, he winked at Danna and shouted back into the house, "Mother, we have visitors!" The elderly man's face broke into an almost childlike grin as he shook both Jered and Danna's hands, welcoming us all into his home and their life. Shame filled my heart, and I whispered fervently, "I'm sorry, Lord. Please forgive me and clean my filthy, angry heart."

We stayed for hours, eating the cookies we had made, reading the kids' books, and listening to stories of our neighbors' own children and grandchildren, who no longer came home and rarely called because they were too busy being successful in life. Jered looked up at me as if to say, "I told you!" When we stood to leave, the now friendly, mild-mannered couple said, "Such lovely children. You should have more! By the way, it's so nice to have such a dependable watchdog nearby. Please come back." We did and soon became friends.

My kids looked past the couple's gruff exterior, sensing their need and, in childlike love, deciding to meet it...despite their clueless mother. Because they did, I learned an important lesson in dealing with difficult people. When you meet a simple need, you may discover it was concealing a much deeper need. That is not the end of the story. A few weeks later, Mr. Smith had a heart attack, and Dan was able to visit him in the hospital and share Christ with him. Because my children reached out and loved someone who seemed to be unlovable, a man's heart was turned to the God of my children's love. Jered and Danna loved their neighbor, just as the Good Samaritan loved his:

> "A man was going down from Jerusalem to Jericho, and fell among robbers, and they stripped him and beat him, and went away leaving him half dead. And by chance, a priest was going down on that road, and when he saw him, he passed by on the other side. Likewise, a Levite also, when he came to the place and saw him, passed by on the other side. But a Samaritan, who was on a journey, came upon him; and when he saw him, he felt compassion, and came to him and bandaged up his wounds, pouring oil and wine on them; and he put him on his own beast, and brought

him to an inn and took care of him. On the next day he took out two denarii and gave them to the innkeeper and said, 'Take care of him; and whatever more you spend, when I return I will repay you.' Which of these three do you think proved to be a neighbor to the man who fell into the robbers' hands?" And he said, 'The one who showed mercy toward him." Then Jesus said to him, "Go and do the same" (Luke 10:30-37 NASB).

The story of the Good Samaritan is one of the most familiar passages in all of Scripture. It is a parable, an earthly story with a heavenly lesson. Jesus tells this parable in response to a question asked him by a Jewish lawyer. "What must I do to inherit eternal life?" the successful young truth-seeker inquired. Seeing his heart, Jesus told him the two things he must do—the two things the lawyer would find it hardest to do. He must love God completely, and his neighbor as himself. The lawyer didn't like that answer, because he lived by the law and wanted that law to be his ticket to heaven. This "loving your neighbor" business sounded too messy and too costly, requiring too much personal responsibility. However, Jesus told the lawyer that keeping the law—God's law and man's law—wasn't enough. Thinking he could find a loophole, the lawyer slyly asked, "Who is my neighbor?" Jesus' answer to that question is the parable of the Good Samaritan. Its message is clear—compassion is not just for the easy-to-love people, but for the not-so-easy-to-love sandpaper person as well. This is an impossible task outside of the supernatural power of God working in and through us. How can we become people of compassion, loving and getting along with people who rub us the wrong way?

DECISION 1: SEE THE NEED

A Samaritan, who was on a journey, came upon him; and...he saw him (Luke 10:33 NASB).

Needy people are everywhere. Some are easy to spot, while others bury their needs deeply, unseen and unmet, locking away each dreadful memory. To be compassionate, we must learn to open our eyes and look for both the obvious and the obscure needs around us. Paul, a man of great compassion, describes the steps we can take to develop compassion in our own lives: "We ask you, brothers and sisters, encourage the people who are afraid. Help those who are weak. Be patient with everyone" (1 Thessalonians 5:14 NCV).

> I wonder just how many sandpaper people are, in fact, angels sent by God. How many angels have we missed because we were too busy to see them?

Every day, needs parade in front of our eyes, but we fail to see them, I believe, for two main reasons. The first reason is, we're too busy. We have schedules to keep. Each morning we don spiritual blinders that will enable us, for the sake of time management, to ignore the hurting people in our path—lonely, desperate people who just need a smile or word of encouragement. If you are like me, I am often guilty of viewing these people as intrusions, interruptions in my very important schedule. In reality, I suspect these uninvited guests are God's divine arrangements, sandpaper people in need of compassion. Hebrews 13:2 is poignant: "Do not forget to entertain strangers, for by so doing some have unwittingly entertained angels" (NKJV). I wonder just how many sandpaper people are, in fact, angels sent by God. How many angels have we missed because we were too busy to see them?

A second reason we fail to see the needs of those around us is, we simply don't care enough. A harsh statement, I know. But the truth is, we do the things in life that are important to us. Jesus says if we love God right, we will naturally love each other right. Compassion is directly related to the health of our personal relationship with Jesus Christ. In the book of 1 John, we find a clear and simple picture of compassion at work—"Whoever does not love does not know God, because God is love" (4:8). "If people say, 'I love God,' but hate their brothers or sisters, they are liars. Those who do not love their brothers and sisters, whom they have seen, cannot love God, whom they have never seen" (4:20 ncv).

We can be very religious and still not care enough. The Levite and the priest saw the wounded man lying in the road and passed him by. Both men were on their way home from church, returning from their Temple duties in Jerusalem to Jericho, the second-largest city of Judea. Jericho was a city filled with thousands of priests and Levites. I'm sure the two men had good reasons for not stopping. After all, they had been serving God at the Temple all week long and were anxious to get home to their families. It was also possible that the same bandits who had assaulted the wounded man could still be hanging around, looking for their next victim! How could they serve God if they were attacked and wounded by bandits? On top of that, it was a busy road and someone would eventually come along and help the man. And he was probably beyond help anyway.

Every day, sandpaper people are discarded on the side of the road, wounded and bleeding. It is so much easier just to walk on by, relegating our responsibility to someone else—anyone else. The way we care for one another and help the difficult people no one else will touch should be an illustration of God's all-inclusive and impartial love.

> I was hungry
>> And you formed a humanities club
>> To discuss my hunger.
> I was imprisoned
>> And you went to your chapel
>> To pray for my release!

I was naked
    And you debated the morality of my appearance.
I was sick
    And you knelt and thanked God for your health.
I was homeless
    And you delivered a sermon
    On the shelter of God's love.
I was lonely
    And you left me alone
    To attend church.
You seem so close to God
    But I am still very hungry, and lonely, and cold!
                                        —Author unknown

Sometimes, we are just too busy being religious to see the need. Compassion always sees the need.

DECISION 2: FEEL THEIR PAIN!

He felt compassion (Luke 10:33 NASB).

Compassion is a key word in 2 Corinthians used 29 times in that letter. It can be defined as "called to one's side to help."

It was Easter Sunday, and I was sitting in the sanctuary waiting for the worship service to begin. Anticipating a large crowd, I arrived early to drop Jered off in the nursery, one of his favorite places to go since every nursery worker doted on him. As the choir filed in, a friend slipped into the pew beside me and said, "I think you need to go to the nursery. Something is wrong with Jered." Jumping up, I leapt over legs, toes, and pews as I raced to the nursery and my son.

I was not prepared for what I saw. In a far corner, lying on his favorite red mat, was Jered, staring at the ceiling, silent and rigid. As I bent over him, searching those beautiful blue eyes, huge tears slid down his chubby cheeks as he flew into my arms, sobbing. You have to understand—as a baby, Jered cried only when he was hungry, wet, or sick. He always seemed to be smiling, happy, and contented. Something was obviously very wrong. I kissed his forehead. No fever. I checked his diaper. Dry and clean. The snack box I had packed for him earlier that morning was empty. I had no idea what had broken my son's heart, but I certainly intended to find out.

Just then, Mrs. Giles, Jered's favorite nursery worker, drew me aside and said, "Let me tell you what happened. We had a new little girl in the nursery today. It was her first time in a church nursery—ever. When her parents left, she immediately began screaming and wouldn't stop. Jered came running and wrapped his arms around her, but she pushed him away. He then brought her his bottle, but she hurled it across the room and continued screaming. Desperate to help her, he found his diaper bag and fished out "Turtle."

Turtle was a small, green-and-blue stuffed turtle we had given Jered several months earlier when he was in the hospital, seriously ill with the croup. From the moment Jered saw Turtle, they were inseparable. He slept with Turtle clutched tightly in one hand, ate with Turtle sitting in his lap, and carefully tucked Turtle in his diaper bag whenever we left the house. Turtle was his most precious possession and was an invaluable source of comfort to him.

Mrs. Giles continued, "I couldn't believe Jered was willing to give Turtle to a stranger, but he tried." The crying child took one look at Turtle and threw it in Jered's face. Stunned, he picked up Turtle, dusted it off, and lay down on the mat, refusing to move, the stuffed animal clutched tightly in his arms. Then I knew. I knew Jered couldn't stand to see the little girl in pain and was determined to help. When he couldn't, he retreated, waiting for someone else to help. That's compassion.

Compassion is empathy, not just sympathy! When it comes to dealing with sandpaper people, we mistakenly equate compassion with "fixing" them. Genuine compassion is first able to feel their pain. I believe one of the reasons we encounter and are commanded to deal with difficult people is because the more pain we experience, the more compassionate we will be! We must learn to use our pain in the right way, not lashing out, but looking within to share the pain of others. There is a choice in every pain, an opportunity in every trial. Pain makes us focus inward or outward. It makes us martyrs or merciful. The choice is ours.

The Samaritan chose to use his pain and help the injured man. He understood the man's pain because of the pain in his own life. The Jews hated all Samaritans. The man lying on the road was a Jew. There was no logical reason for this Samaritan to rearrange his plans and spend his money to help this "enemy" or "sandpaper person" in need. But compassion doesn't look for reasons or search out limitations. It searches for opportunity! The Samaritan had a choice, just as we have a choice every time we are confronted with a need. We must adjust our thinking to understand that abrasive people are needy people. We can either ignore the need, or we can meet the need by giving away part of the comfort God has given us.

> Praise be to the God and Father of our Lord Jesus Christ, the Father of compassion and the God of all comfort, who comforts us in all our troubles, so that we can comfort those in any trouble with the comfort we ourselves have received from God (2 Corinthians 1:3-4).

> Share each other's troubles and problems, and in this way obey the law of Christ (Galatians 6:2 NLT).

If we can't prevent pain, we can at least lighten the load with compassion. Alan Redpath wrote, "You can never lighten the load unless you have first felt the pressure in your own soul." To develop compassion, we must be willing to feel the pain of others, responding as if it were our own.

DECISION 3: TAKE IMMEDIATE ACTION!

> He came to him and bandaged up his wounds, pouring oil and wine on them; and he put him on his own beast, and brought him to an inn and took care of him (Luke 10:34 NASB).

The Jewish lawyer wanted to discuss "neighbor" in a general way, a less costly and personal way. Instead, Jesus forced him to consider a specific man with specific needs, pointing out that the Samaritan met the needs of the injured man in specific ways. We often use the excuse that we don't have the resources to help someone in need. Notice that the Samaritan used all of the resources he had, the *only* resources he had—and they were enough. With oil and wine, the Samaritan cleansed the Jewish man's wounds and put him on his own beast, which meant the Samaritan would have to walk. If that wasn't enough, he took this Jewish stranger to an inn and made sure he received the care he needed! In verse 35, we discover that the Samaritan gave the innkeeper two denarii, which is the equivalent of two days' wages.

In other words, the Samaritan went the extra mile and did it right. He could have simply bandaged the wounded man and left him for another Jew to pick up by the side of the busy road, where others would certainly be traveling that day. But the Samaritan didn't hesitate. He didn't wait. He took immediate action and met the need. When it comes to seeing and meeting needs, 1 John 3:17-18 makes our responsibility clear: "Suppose someone has enough to live and sees a brother or sister in need, but does not help. Then God's love is not living in that person. We should love people not only with words and talk, but by our actions and true caring" (NCV).

Compassion says that short-term care is up to me. I must use my resources and get personally involved. I must step into the middle of the mess. That is what genuine compassion naturally does. When someone in need crosses our path or we have a burden for someone, there is always a reason. God has already equipped us and provided everything we need to meet that need or ease that burden. Don't call the church office or local charity. Do something!

People in pain are often unable to ask for help because they are emotionally paralyzed by their pain. Since we may not know exactly what to do, we do nothing at all. But it doesn't take much.

Just one tiny seed of compassion goes a long way. A gentle hug, a note or phone call to let them know you are praying, a meal or an errand run can mean the world to a person in pain.

As I mentioned earlier, in 1995 I went through a two-year battle with clinical depression. My first book, *Coming Out of the Dark*, came out of this experience, chronicling my journey from darkness to light. At the time, my husband was the pastor of the large and fast-growing church in South Florida I described previously. I was extremely involved and highly visible, but I was also a woman filled with pride, desperately clinging to self-sufficiency as my world crumbled around my feet. I was usually the strong one, dispensing hope and wisdom to others who found themselves at the bottom of a deep, dark pit. Now I, the strong one, couldn't get out of bed. If I was dressed by the time my children got home from school, it was a good day.

I was the director of our very large and very active women's ministry, but suddenly the smallest choices sent me spiraling into panic attacks. I had a very active speaking schedule and the bigger the crowd, the better I liked it. Now, crowds overwhelmed me to the point that I found it hard to attend even one worship service. I was in excruciating emotional pain but refused to ask for or accept any offer of help. It didn't matter. The people of Flamingo Road Church stepped in and helped anyway. They demonstrated the eternal impact and transforming power of compassion.

Church members delivered meals, picked up my children from school, bought my groceries, and delivered my dry cleaning. Women cleaned my house and did my laundry, expecting nothing in return. Deacons and lay pastors "guarded" me when I did manage to attend church, making sure I was safe from anyone demanding my attention or those who wanted to know every gory detail of my struggle. My sister and brother-in-law made a surprise visit to help me through the Thanksgiving holidays, while many prayed and fasted for my recovery. My husband came home each day to feed and bathe the children before putting them to bed. He would then change clothes and settle in on the couch beside me to listen as I poured out my fear and pain, night after night—to hold me when I cried and love me when I was so very unlovable.

Compassion saved me—the compassion of God and the compassion of those who made the choice to get involved with me, which meant getting involved with my pain. I will be forever grateful for them and for the pit of depression that taught me what love is all about and how it is lived out in compassion. And I know that people are sometimes hard to help. I certainly was.

The story is told of two Cub Scouts whose younger brother had fallen into the lake. They rushed home, panicked and crying all the way, desperately hoping to find their mother. As they fell into her arms, one of the boys sobbed out the story. "We tried to give him artificial respiration, but he kept getting up and walking away!" That would be me too—and so many others in desperate need of someone who is willing to step into their lives, uninvited, to meet a need and give help. Don't let the carefully erected wall of someone in pain keep you from compassion. Even when someone is hard to help, compassion doesn't wait or simply give up. Compassion takes action!

DECISION 4: MAKE A LONG-TERM PLAN

On the next day he took out two denarii and gave them to the innkeeper and said, "Take care of him" (Luke 10:35 NASB).

We must learn to live life with margins, setting aside time for those unexpected opportunities through which compassion can work. In other words, we should leave room in schedules for divine interruptions. Plan for them, always remembering that His agenda is the one we need to be concerned about, not our own. The psalmist says it well: "In his heart a man plans his course, but the LORD determines his steps" (Psalm 16:9 NCV).

Be wise, asking for God's discernment and direction in meeting the needs of others. As with any gift from God, there are pitfalls that accompany compassion. We can be so busy meeting the needs of others that we fail to meet our own needs or the needs of our family. In doing so, we lose sight of the main thing. Life is filled with emotional black holes and sandpaper people running around, taking up emotional room, and wasting emotional energy that could be better spent on those who truly are in need, those who will respond to compassion and love. We must be good stewards of the emotional energy and eternal investments we make, constantly seeking discernment in order to determine God's priorities and plans. We must strike a fragile balance, which requires constant adjustment and fine-tuning as we reach out to others. In some cases, we can become a crutch, standing in the way of God's higher plan. (Remember the story of Sherry and me?) Then there are those who really don't want to have their needs met. They just want your time and attention.

After you have stopped the bleeding, make a long-term plan! Notice that the Samaritan was *not* the long-term plan. He had a referral system and outside resources on which he could count. We must always balance compassion with responsibility. It's important to notice that the Samaritan was "on a journey"—he had somewhere to go and a destination in mind. Judging from the way he ministered to the wounded man on the side of the road, I would say the Samaritan was a man with a purpose and a plan. Compassion never eliminates the big picture. Compassion makes a long-term plan!

DECISION 5: ALWAYS FOLLOW UP

Whatever more you spend, when I return I will repay you (Luke 10:35 NASB).

The Samaritan demonstrates just how far-reaching true compassion is! He promised to return. He did not say "if" I return but "when" I return. Follow-up brings accountability into the picture, something that is very important when dealing with a sandpaper person. Because they constantly drive people away, sandpaper people rarely have anyone who sticks with them, holding them accountable for the way they handle relationships and life itself. Compassion holds the promise, "I will keep caring." Honestly, it is sometimes easier just to "fix" them in order to be rid of them! True compassion goes beyond a solution...all the way to restoration!

The Samaritan also promised to be available. "I will repay you," he told the innkeeper. At the heart of compassion is commitment as well as flexibility. One lesson we are destined to learn from the difficult relationships in life is the lesson of flexibility. The Samaritan didn't really know on the front end what the ultimate cost of caring for the Jewish man would be. He wasn't worried. "Whatever more you spend" he promised to pay. Every investment in people involves risk, but the return is always proportionate to the risk—the greater the risk, the greater the return.

Yes, compassion can indeed be messy business. This point is well made in the story of a farmer who was out plowing his field one beautiful spring morning. The spring thaw had just occurred, so muddy ruts covered the entire field. While he worked, his tractor became stuck in the mud. The harder he tried to free it, the deeper he was stuck. Finally, he walked over to his neighbor's farm and asked for help. When the neighbor came over to assess the situation, he shook his head ruefully and announced, "Well, it doesn't look good. But I tell you what I'll do. I'll try my hardest to pull you out. But if we can't get that tractor to budge, I'll sit in the mud with ya until more help comes along." Have you tried "mud-sitting" with a friend? It just might be compassion at its best! Dealing with sandpaper people can sometimes leave us a little dirty, but when we emerge from the mess of ministry, we are beautifully dressed, according to the words of Paul: "As God's chosen people, holy and dearly loved, clothe yourselves with compassion, kindness, humility, gentleness and patience" (Colossians 3:12).

Compassion at work always honors God and draws people to Him. Take the innkeeper, for example. I am certain he was both amazed and curious as he watched the Samaritan care for the

Jewish man, a known enemy. In human terms, it just didn't make sense. The Samaritan's actions must have seemed illogical. Think about how the injured man must have felt when he woke to find an enemy had saved his life. Compassion is most powerful when it is shown to an enemy and is least expected. The sandpaper people in your world do not need condemnation. They need compassion! The sandpaper people in your world do not need a sermon. They need a hand of compassion. The question is, are you willing for that hand to be yours?

⌒

To the thieves, this Jew was merely a victim they could exploit. They attacked him, leaving him to die. To the priest and Levite, he was just a nuisance they avoided. But to the Samaritan, the Jew was a neighbor in need of love and care. In compassion, the Samaritan took care of him.

"Which of these three do you think proved to be a neighbor to the man who fell into the robbers' hands?" And he said, "The one who showed mercy toward him." Then Jesus said to him, "Go and do the same."
Luke 10:36-37

Music: sandpaper scrapers. A scraper is a simple rhythm instrument. Notches are carved into a gourd, bamboo, shell, bone, wood, or other material. When a stick or other hard object is drawn over the notches, it makes a sound. The most common form of scraper is a *guiro*, which is made from a gourd. It also has small rocks inside that make a rainlike sound.

Supplies:
- Use a sanding block when hand-sanding.
- two small blocks of pine or plywood, approximately 1″ x 5″ x 6″
- sandpaper (two different grits are best)
- thumbtacks (colorful ones look nice)
- scissors
- wooden or plastic thread spools and glue (or small cabinet knobs with screws)

Steps:
1. Cover one side of each block with sandpaper, and fold over the edges. Cut slits in each corner so the sandpaper will fold neatly around the block.

2. Secure sandpaper around the edges of the blocks with thumbtacks. Trim any excess.

3. Glue spools (or attach cabinet knobs) to the side of the blocks opposite the sandpaper.[7]

Art: sandpaper rubbings. Preschoolers love to feel the different textures in their environment. When a child makes sandpaper rubbings, he enjoys seeing the texture as well.

Materials: Large crayons, thin paper, sandpaper

Directions: Place paper on object covered with sandpaper and rub with crayon. Vary the pressure applied to demonstrate different textures.[8]

Eight

Be Peaceful:
Wage Peace

*Those who do not control themselves
are like a city whose walls are broken down.*
Proverbs 25:28 NCV

We ARE EMOTIONAL CRITTERS, created by God with the capacity for strong emotions! Like any gift from God's hand, our emotions can be used for good or misused for ill. Sandpaper people not only have an uncanny knack for knowing where emotional buttons are located, they honestly think it is their purpose in life to push every single one of them. Our first reaction to the incessant and calculated button-pushing of a sandpaper person is usually angry retaliation.

But God calls us to a peaceful resolution. When it comes to difficult relationships, He does not want or expect us to declare war. We are to control our emotions instead of allowing them to control us. Paul writes in Romans 12:18, "If it is possible, as far as it depends on you, live at peace with everyone." When it comes to relationships, especially the challenging relationships, we need to set our mind on peace—not winning.

In every relationship, God's desire is for us to wage peace. What is even more amazing to me is the fact that God calls us to wage peace with even the roughest, most abrasive, most anger-producing sandpaper people who come our way. A formidable task, since every sandpaper person I have ever known comes complete with a set agenda that aims for emotional eruptions and creates constant relationships upheavals! They love a good fight, live to provoke angry reactions, and are fierce warriors determined to win every battle initiated by their downright irritating personalities.

However, combat is impossible when the enemy has laid down his weapons and chosen peace. As I headed to the grocery store one day for my dreaded weekly shopping trip, I was wrestling with a bad attitude. You have to understand that I always have and probably always will despise grocery shopping. Nevertheless, on this particular morning, I vowed to choose joy, turning my focus to the balmy Florida day before me. I had it all under control— until I pulled into the grocery-store parking lot.

Every South Florida resident was in that parking lot, frantically searching for a place to park—and they were not happy! After circling the crowded parking lot several times, I spotted an empty space right by the entrance! God does answer prayer. I made a beeline for "my" parking space. Just as I turned to pull in, an older lady boldly stepped into that prized space and, with the authority of a veteran parking-space hunter, dramatically held up her left hand, signaling me to stop right where I was. With her right hand, this self-designated traffic director began frantically motioning to a man I assumed was her husband as he circled the parking lot in his impressively large black car. I suddenly realized she was saving "my" spot for him with her very life as collateral. Of all the nerve! What incredible gall! Parking spaces are a serious matter to me— and in my mind can sometimes be considered a sign of God's favor on me, His preferred child! Evidently, I was not the only one who felt that way.

In the midst of my simmering, soon-to-explode anger, a still, small voice reminded me I had a choice to make. I really hated surrendering my anger to Him, but the thought of having to apologize to that ridiculous woman for running over her with my car was more than my mind could conceive and my stomach could handle. I quickly decided that if she was willing to risk her life for a grocery-store parking space, she deserved to have it. Unfortunately, the driver behind me did not agree and whipped her pint-sized car into the sought after space just in front of the man in his impressively large black car, barely missing the horrified traffic-controlling woman as she hastily jumped up on the sidewalk out of the minicar's deadly path. I decided to watch the scene unfold—or explode. Crude gestures and loud, repulsive words filled the air. Some I understood. Some I had never heard and didn't care to understand. Threats were exchanged, along with inflated promises of retribution. Finally, the parking-lot security officer stepped in and, with great finesse, invited the belligerent drivers to do their shopping at the grocery store down the street. I loved that man! And I got "my" parking space after all.

The entire scenario reminded me that we live in a world filled with angry people who are constantly rubbing each other the wrong way. Sandpaper people. While it is true that everyone is angry from time to time, it is just as true that everyone can learn to effectively control and manage their anger. When dealing with a sandpaper person, we must never allow ourselves to become the opponent or the enemy. I know what you are thinking. That is easy to say, but in the heat of the moment, very hard to do. You are exactly right! Therefore, we need to prepare *now* for the angry circumstances and people headed our way. Allow me to offer several steps we can take in dealing with the anger that sandpaper people often provoke.

STEP 1: RECOGNIZE THE POWER OF ANGER!

Anger is an emotional warning light, alerting us to the fact that something is wrong. We may be hurt or frustrated, rejected or wronged. Simply put, something has changed, and we don't like it! Anger itself is not sin. In Ephesians 4:26 we find Paul's simple but very clear directive: "In your anger, do not sin." Paul is indicating that God created us with the capacity for anger. Therefore, it is possible to be angry and yet not sin! The challenge is to learn how to express anger correctly, harnessing it and molding it into a tool for good, instead of allowing it to imprison its victim.

Sandpaper people often don't know how to deal with their own anger, much less the anger they cause. As a result, they mishandle the emotion. Mishandled anger always leads to emotional destruction and broken relationships. Proverbs 27:4 describes this damage: "Anger is cruel and destroys like a flood" (NCV). Mishandled anger is not only destructive, it is obstructive—and many times, it gets in the way of God's justice. Revenge belongs solely in the hands of God—"It is mine to avenge; I will repay" (Deuteronomy 32:35).

Several years ago, a family friend showed up at our front door with an electric sander for Dan, encouraging him to try woodworking as a stress-relieving hobby. My husband not only developed a love for woodworking but also created some beautiful pieces of furniture in the process. Being a supportive wife and the main benefactor of his newfound hobby, I felt a responsibility to encourage him in any way I could.

For every birthday or special event, I bought him a power tool and strategically distributed a list of wanted but yet-to-be-purchased tools for friends and family members to consider as a gift choice. (I know—I, too, have always cringed at each "You cannot possibly please me in selecting a present, so here are the things I want for Christmas" gift list. However, in this case, it seemed to make perfect sense). Within a year, Dan was enjoying an impressive collection of tools—which he proudly displayed in the garage—and I was enjoying several new pieces of handmade furniture—which I proudly displayed in the house. Without a doubt, however, the most precious by-product of Dan's new hobby was watching Jered, then six, as he worked untiringly beside his daddy.

Day after day, they headed out to the garage for some "daddy time." Dan built a workbench just for Jered beside his own larger workstation. Jered had his own toolbox just like his dad's and inherited a hodgepodge of tools from his dad's collection. I could hear them singing, laughing, hammering, and buzzing away happily for hours, creating not only an impressive assortment of unique wooden creations, but a prized collection of father–son memories as well. Since Dan especially loved working with pine, he kept a good supply on hand, piling leftover or unused pieces in Jered's wood box for his own special projects. There was one problem. Jered was completely fascinated by those power tools and was constantly sneaking into the garage, hoping his dad had left one plugged in for him to use. We had to come up with a solution—and fast!

Christmas was just around the corner, so Dan and I doggedly trudged from store to store until we found the ideal gift for Jered, the perfect solution to the power tool dilemma. It was the cutest little workbench, with its own set of brightly colored plastic tools. It even included a genuine leather tool belt and a pair of plastic eye goggles! It was perfect! We carefully wrapped and strategically placed the workbench under the tree, anticipating the look on our son's face when he opened his "workshop in a box."

On Christmas morning, every gift had been opened with the exception of the strangely wrapped present tucked into the back branches of the Christmas tree, just waiting to be claimed by the resident junior carpenter. Finally, with utter delight, Jered ripped away the brightly colored wrapping paper, tossing it in the air like a holiday snowstorm, revealing our "perfect" present. Time stood still as we waited for his ecstatic reaction. It did not come. Questioningly picking up the plastic red hammer, he conducted a thorough examination of each and every tool before he turned to us, his face a picture of disappointment and determination, to issue the verdict. "These are baby tools. I can't use them because I'm not a baby. I have to use real tools like Daddy's tools."

With an air of finality, Jered turned on his heels, heading straight for the garage and certain danger. Dan scrambled to his feet and followed him outside as I began praying for just the right words of explanation. Kneeling beside him, Dan picked up the sander and gently said, "Son, I know you are disappointed with the plastic tools Mom and I bought for you. I'm sorry you don't like them, and believe me—I understand why you love the power tools. They really are cool and fun! But you need to listen carefully, Son. This is very important. These power tools were made to fit Daddy's hands." Holding out his big, daddy-sized hands and placing Jered's small hands in them, Dan pointed out the difference. He went on to explain that, in little hands, the tools could be destructive and even harmful, but in Daddy's hands, they were productive tools and could build and create wonderful things.

Revenge was never intended for our hands. It belongs solely in the hands of God. When an abrasive person comes into our lives, inflicting pain and wreaking emotional havoc, it's easy to build a case for retaliation and revenge against them, thinking they will turn and run if we "show them who's boss." We need to realize that when we choose to strike back at a sandpaper person, we are setting the stage for explosive disaster. Our human revenge destroys, while God's revenge brings justice and restoration. Anger is powerful and can even be deadly in the hands of sandpaper people, as well as in the hands of anyone who tries to take revenge on a sandpaper person. Anger—in the wrong hands, handled the wrong way—destroys.

STEP 2: LEARN HOW TO DEAL WITH ANGER

From time to time, every relationship will require a response to anger-filled words, attitudes, or actions. When it comes to the relationships we have with people who rub us the wrong way, sparks fly easily, igniting a relationship war and battle of wills. In those tense moments when it seems there is no choice we actually do always have a choice in how we respond. The life of Nehemiah offers a wonderful example of making the right choice in the face of anger. He models perfectly how to control anger and deal with sandpaper people—God's way.

Nehemiah had come back to Jerusalem from a high position in the Persian court to supervise the rebuilding of the Jerusalem walls. A delegation of Hebrews who had come with him, hoping to make a profit, took advantage of the poor by enslaving widows and children. The sick and those unable to defend themselves were also at the mercy of these Hebrews, who robbed and terrorized them.

Nehemiah was angry, to put it mildly—but in the grip of anger, he still models for us the right way to deal with that anger and the sandpaper people who caused it. "When I heard their outcry and these charges, I was very angry. I pondered them in my mind and then accused the nobles and officials. So I called together a large meeting to deal with them" (Nehemiah 5:6-7). The words of Nehemiah offer three ways to deal with anger.

Admit We Are Angry

Nehemiah was viciously honest about his feelings. "When I heard their outcry and these charges, I was very angry." Many times we refuse to admit we are angry, thinking that if we deny our anger, it will disappear and we won't have to deal with it at all. Our solution of camouflaging or disguising anger is really no solution at all. Sarcasm, gossip, complaining, criticism, or aggressive attitudes are common masks that anger wears. Sandpaper people carry trunkloads of personality masks in order to be who they think the current audience wants them to be. When they fail to live up to expectations from any source, including their own heart, frustration bubbles to the surface like a sure-to-erupt volcano. Allowing anger to simmer on the back burner of our emotions is like sitting on a keg of dynamite while striking matches, just for fun. One day, that keg of anger will surely explode, wreaking havoc and throwing emotional shrapnel when and where it's least expected. Irrational behavior and destructive actions will be the result.

It was testimony night at the small country church. In the middle of the pastor's sermon, a lady jumped to her feet, turned to the congregation, and announced, "I have something I need to confess. We are living in a wicked, evil world where sin is on every hand. I've had a terrible fight with that old devil all week, and he has made me so angry." Her husband, who was sitting by her side, protested, "Hey! It's not all my fault. She's tough to live with too!" No one, including sandpaper people, can "make" us angry without our permission. We must not give it.

Too often, we are guilty of trying to stuff anger into some secluded or hidden corner of our emotional bank account, hoping it will magically evaporate without a trace left behind. Nehemiah models a higher plan. "I was angry!" Nehemiah minced no words, confessing in an honest and transparent admission. To deal with anger, we must be willing to acknowledge the presence of that anger; not because God is surprised by our anger, but because in taking that first step of admitting we are angry, we initiate the healing process.

I sometimes wonder if God doesn't allow a steady stream of sandpaper people to flow through our lives to push limits that are already strained, consume emotional energy we don't have to spare and, ultimately, to expose the true state of our hearts. Why does a loving God allow sandpaper people to come? The answer is a cornerstone of relationship principles: because His ways are higher than our ways and because He is more committed to our character than to our comfort. The certainty of 1 Chronicles 29:17 is motivation enough to be authentic and transparent with our emotions: "I know, my God, that you examine our hearts and rejoice when you find integrity there" (NLT). To deal with anger we must have emotional integrity before God and man! Being real in order to be right is not only a foundational truth of inner well-being but an important step of obedience to God as well. Sandpaper people struggle with this step and are uncomfortable with transparency because it strips away any façade or pretense of hypocrisy and their real identity is exposed. The result is shallow and meaningless relationships.

Delay Our Response

Nehemiah writes, "I pondered them in my mind." The word *ponder* means "to deliberately examine, to carefully contemplate or accurately weigh something." To ponder anger can best be described by the idea of a revolving emotional display, in which the anger is contemplated, examined, and viewed from all sides. In other words, when anger strikes, we need to gain control of our thoughts and emotions and then examine them before we express them. Proverbs 19:11 explains, "People with good sense restrain their anger" (NLT). Harnessing anger is controlling anger instead of allowing it to control us.

Sometimes anger should be postponed for a time. The truth of Proverbs 29:11 is very basic: "A stupid man gives free rein to his anger; a wise man waits and lets it grow cool" (ICB). When a sandpaper person makes us furious, we must deliberately choose the right response. In reality, we need to make that choice before the circumstance ever demands it. A foolish man assumes he can handle any situation without becoming angry. Sandpaper people count on that assumption, knowing that when we are consumed with anger, we are capable of anything. On the other hand, a wise man waits and lets his anger grow cool to the point where it can be handled safely and correctly. In dealing with sandpaper people, we need to cool it!

When my daughter was about six years old, she and I were engaged in a battle of wills. It was very simple. I wanted her to go

> ama, I can't talk right now. My mad is way too big!" Danna was taking the time to "cool it." We should do the same.

to sleep. She, however, had other plans for the evening, none of which included sleep. When she realized I wasn't going to give in, she stomped to her room, furious with her unreasonable and demanding mother. A few minutes passed before I went to make peace. As I slowly opened the door, making sure I wouldn't be met by a flying object, I saw Danna sitting on her bed, arms crossed, teeth clenched, big, brown eyes still flashing with anger. "Danna, let's talk about this," I began. Immediately, her response came, aloof and firm but profound: "Mama, I can't talk right now. My mad is way too big!" Danna was taking the time to "cool it." We should do the same.

When Jesus saw the money changers in His Father's temple, I believe His mad was too big! I can just see Him as He marched toward those men, ready to help them see the error of their ways, righteous indignation fueling every step. Suddenly He stopped, stepped over to the side, and began braiding a whip. The Son of God did not step aside to braid that whip because He had taken "Whip Braiding 101." Jesus was "cooling it," I think—stepping aside until He could control His anger instead of allowing it to control Him. Then with harnessed anger, He drove out every sandpaper person in sight.

The truth is, the longer you hold your temper the more it improves. If, as it appears, Jesus had to take time to get His anger under control, we will as well. I love the fact that Jesus chose to braid a whip, a tedious task requiring concentration and focus. Harnessing anger always takes concentration and focus. We also need to take note that braiding that whip was a physical task in the midst of a mental war. Harnessing anger can often be accomplished simply by finding some physical task in which to engage so that anger can be "worked out," rather than have free rein.

Learning to control anger is a crucial life lesson—one we need to master and pass on to our children. Up until my young-adult years, I had a huge temper. It took very little to make me furious. In moments of anger, I would slam doors, hurl objects across the room, and yell a lot! I don't remember anyone telling me what to do with my anger—until I totally surrendered my heart to God. And believe me, *He* had *plenty* to say! "Everyone should be quick to listen, slow to speak and slow to become angry, for man's anger does not bring about the righteous life that God desires" (James 1:19-20).

As the years went by, I married and became the mother of two amazing children who, unfortunately, inherited my huge temper. It was now my responsibility to train Jered and Danna in the ways of God, including ways of controlling anger! I prayed continually that God would not only teach *me* practical methods of managing my own anger but that He would enable me to teach my children to control their anger as well. That is how the "mad board" was created.

When Jered was nine years old, we realized that he frequently struggled with his little sister. She had discovered each and every one of her brother's emotional buttons and delighted in pushing them. His frustration grew until the day he retaliated. My husband and I came up with the "mad board." Dan cut a two-by-four piece of plywood and started 50 or more nails into it. He wrote "Jered's Mad Board" on it and handed it to his curious son. He explained that whenever Jered became frustrated or angry with his sister, he should pick up his junior-sized hammer and drive nails into the board instead of driving his fist into his sister's face.

Over the next few months, we watched Jered drive a lot of nails into a lot of wood, learning that anger can be managed. Today, as a senior in college, Jered is an even-tempered young man who has found constructive ways to manage his anger. In fact, over the years, our whole family has learned some techniques for controlling anger:

1. Pray for the person or circumstance that caused your anger.
2. Exercise strenuously for 20 minutes.
3. Play a solo game of basketball or jog a mile.
4. Run an errand in order to have a short, silent "retreat."

5. Take a hot shower or bath.

6. Breathe in to the count of nine. Hold your breath for a count of nine and exhale to the count of nine. Repeat three times.

7. Memorize five Bible verses on anger and speak them aloud when angry.

8. Journal your feelings. (Even children can do this.)

9. Take a 15-minute walk, breathing deeply, taking long, quick strides.

10. Buy a punching bag and use it to release destructive anger.

The people around us want to see what happens when life pushes our buttons and anger puts the squeeze on our emotions. While God created us with the emotions, it is our responsibility to control them instead of allowing them to control us. When your sandpaper person has once again scraped through your resistance and the temptation to respond in anger threatens to overtake you, do what Jesus did. Stop—grab that harness and take control of your anger.

Dismiss Our Anger

At times, the right response to anger is no response at all. We should simply dismiss it, or "put it out of our life," as James advises. "Do not become angry easily, because anger will not help you live the right kind of life God wants. So put out of your life every evil thing and every kind of wrong" (James 1:21 NCV). When anger strikes, we need to stop and ask ourselves some important questions before responding. What is the *real* reason for my anger? Is it truly important, or do I simply want my own way? Will it matter in a year? What action do I need to take or *not* take? Small pots boil over quickly and so do small people! The emotions of sandpaper people are often unstable or volatile, and hurt is imminent. Maturity is the ability to overlook a hurt and then dismiss the anger. Part of a godly discipline is learning to handle and control every God-given emotion, including anger. Some anger should simply be dismissed as unworthy of occupying emotional space or consuming emotional energy.

Resolve Our Anger!

When anger is attached to an important issue, we must resolve that issue. One solution is to postpone anger for a short time, but only to decide if we need to dismiss it or resolve it! Resolving anger is a daily spiritual discipline. "When you are angry, do not sin, and be sure to stop being angry before the end of the day. Do not give the devil a way to defeat you" (Ephesians 4:26-27). When we refuse to address anger, it hardens and takes hold, adhering to our souls and eventually becoming bitterness—one of Satan's favorite strongholds and a place from which he dispenses defeat and loss. Furthermore, when we hold onto anger it becomes an open door for other sins to come pouring into our lives right behind it! Paul warns, "Now is the time to get rid of anger, rage, malicious behavior, slander, and dirty language. Don't lie to each other, for you have stripped off your old evil nature and all its wicked deeds" (Colossians 3:8-9 NLT). Notice the progression of sin. What we deem obscene or beyond our ability to change may begin with one angry emotion we simply refuse to confront and resolve.

Resolving anger requires healthy communication, something sandpaper people know very little about. Therefore, we must be willing to take the lead. Healthy responses to anger are delivered at a low volume. Paul says it well: "Do not be bitter or angry or mad. Never shout angrily or say things to hurt others" (Ephesians 4:31 NCV). No one will hear shouted words. Nothing defuses anger and the possibility of an explosive situation like a soft answer. In Proverbs 15:1, we find the observation that "a soft answer turns away wrath!" (NKJV). In other words, lower the volume!

One Tuesday morning, I was busy preparing to teach our weekly women's Bible study. The morning had not gone as planned, and I was frantically arranging chairs, checking supplies, and trying desperately to keep my heart and spirit in check. When the work was done, I knew I needed to stop, be still, and seek the presence of God before standing up to teach. Pulling a chair into the far corner of the room, I sat quietly, facing the wall, asking the Father to calm and prepare my chaotic heart to share His truth. The solitude was replenishing—but short-lived.

The door burst open, and the husband of one of my group leaders barged into the room, tension oozing from every pore. Obviously he was not happy. Furthermore, I could tell by the look on his reddened face that whatever was wrong was definitely *my* fault! In a thunderous voice, veins popping and eyes bulging, he began to explain the problem, ending his verbal tirade with this question: "Now—what are you going to do about it?" In a rare moment of wisdom, I shut my mouth, slowly stood to my feet, gently put my hand on his shoulder and, smiling my best smile, looked him in the eye. He was stunned. But little did he know the best was yet to be. I then whispered, "I'll tell you what I am going to do. I am going to do whatever it takes to make you happy." The now deflated man stumbled backward as if I had hit him! Catching himself, he plopped into a nearby chair, staring at me as if I were the eighth wonder of the world. I have to admit, I was feeling somewhat wonderful at this point. With astonishment on his face and disbelief in his eyes, the once rabid man now muttered a slightly confused "thank you." Scrambling to his feet, he made a quick exit.

I learned an important lesson that morning. We have a choice about the place we assign our emotions. When Nehemiah postponed his anger, then harnessed it, he told the nobles and officials to return what they had stolen—and they did! Learning to deal with anger is a major life lesson. It impacts us personally and equips us to better deal with sandpaper people.

STEP 3: RESOLVE TO PREVENT ANGER!

In Proverbs 14:16 we find the encouraging adage, "A wise man is cautious and turns away from evil" (NASB). The old saying that an ounce of prevention is worth a pound of cure definitely applies to preventing anger and affects how we handle sandpaper people. In other words, we need to avoid, like the plague, those things—people—circumstances—that are filled with or prone to anger. Anger is contagious. If we spend time with angry people, we will become angry! Sandpaper people have allowed outer circumstances to dictate their inner attitudes; they want others to do the same, and their actions and words invite us to join them in their rage. Proverbs 22:24-25 says clearly, "Don't make friends with quick-tempered people or spend time with those who have bad tempers" (NCV). If we do, we will be just like them.

Another way to prevent anger is to live a balanced life. When the priorities in life are rightly chosen and firmly established, we are less likely to be filled with anger. Stress and constant hurry leave a door open, through which anger and frustration rush, with disappointment and regret on their heels. Proverbs 14:16 describes the results of a life out of control: "A fool is hotheaded and reckless." A lack of balance leads to reckless behavior. Reckless people are rash, wild, and without control. Where there are no boundaries or hedges of protection, there is no control. It's much easier to become frustrated, make foolish choices, and respond in anger when our schedules are overcrowded and our lives are overwhelmed. An unbalanced life is an anger-prone life.

We need to deal with anger in the right way for our own good—but there is another reason, a higher reason for anger management. A pastor was putting in a wooden fence around his backyard. As he hammered away, he noticed a little boy watching him work. The boy didn't say a word, he just watched. The preacher kept working, thinking the little boy would leave, but he didn't! Pleased at the thought of his work being admired, he finally said, "Well, son—trying to pick up some pointers on building?" "No," the young spectator quickly answered. "I'm just waiting to hear what a preacher says when he hits his thumb with a hammer!"

The world is watching, as is every sandpaper person in your life! They are pushing every limit and testing every emotion to see how you will respond. What's really inside will come out. In dealing with the difficult relationships in life, we must learn how to wage peace by dealing with anger.

SANDPAPER 101

How does sandpaper work? Sandpaper works a lot like a saw, chisel, or any other cutting tool. The particles on sandpaper have sharp edges that cut wood the same way a saw blade does. The only real difference is that sandpaper, unlike a saw, can't be sharpened.

Is all sandpaper the same? No. There are two different grades of sandpaper on the market—commercial and industrial. The commercial grade is commonly available at hardware stores and home-project centers. The industrial grade is usually available only through industrial-supply stores. It's made from higher quality materials and is designed to be used in production lines.

What is *grit*? When talking about sandpaper, *grit* is a reference to the number of abrasive particles per inch of sandpaper. The lower the grit the rougher the sandpaper—and the higher the grit, the smoother the sandpaper. Sandpaper is classified by its grit (for example, *150-grit sandpaper*).[9]

Nine

Be Confrontational:
Care Enough to Confront

Faithful are the wounds of a friend.
Proverbs 27:6 NASB

WE ARE BORN HELPLESS. As soon as we are fully conscious, we discover loneliness. God created us to need each other, and to both discover and have that need met in relationships. Throughout Scripture, God repeatedly emphasizes the value and benefits of healthy relationships. However, to my way of thinking, life would be so much easier at times if no one needed us and we needed no one because, honestly, relationships are hard work...especially relationships with sandpaper people.

Difficult relationships and people who rub us the wrong way are often given permanent tickets into our world, tickets that don't always come with escape clauses. Therefore, we must make a choice. We can either learn to get along with our sandpaper people—or retreat into substitute, shallow relationships instead of the deep, meaningful ones God intends us to enjoy. Escape may take the form of working during the hours that should be spent learning to live together in peace. Children fill the void that a difficult spouse refuses to fill. Needs are unmet and desires are numbed in an effort to live peacefully with that sandpaper person. Marriages are filled with conflict and turmoil because one or both marriage partners are sandpaper people, one or both refusing to compromise or surrender. Friendships splinter and workplace relationships disintegrate under the constant emotional hammering we take from people who rub us the wrong way.

I find it almost humorous—*almost*—that sandpaper people rarely see or accept the fact that they are the coarser of the two in any relationship. The abrasive people in life are masters at dodging blame and skirting responsibility for the emotional upheaval that follows them like their own shadow. One of the treasures of a marriage relationship is the learned ability to give and take. Friendships are meant to teach us how to love and trust people on many different levels. The workplace is a laboratory for personality experiments and conflict management. A thread of flexibility runs through the center of every healthy relationship so we can accept those who grate on our nerves while accommodating their quirks and flaws. The problem is that sandpaper people avoid flexibility if possible, afraid that any change will exclude them, which is the very thing they fear most and the one thing their abrasive behavior usually produces. The question then becomes, what part must we play in dealing with these difficult people? How can we come to the table of relationship health and walk away with a cure?

A Basic Need

One of the basic needs of every healthy relationship is the art of confrontation. To confront someone is to meet them head-on in the quest for compromise. Confrontation is a way to pull someone over to the side of the road emotionally for the purpose of resolving conflict, while still promoting peace. Just as God separates who we are from our sin, He calls us to do the same with sandpaper people. We must disconnect who they are from what they do, loving the sinner but hating the sin and looking beyond their weaknesses in search of their strengths.

Most people I know hate confrontation and will do anything to avoid it. But in doing so, they give the impression they are content with the status quo. It is important for us to understand that to sandpaper people, silence is agreement. Sandpaper people take silence as the absence of "no" and the presence of an unspoken "yes."

I suppose the mother of every teenager can relate to the fact that, at some point during those teen years, their precious child will turn into a sandpaper person, complete with fangs and horns. I am just as certain that the *mother* of every teenager is the proud owner of her own set of fangs and horns. However, somebody has to step up and be the adult and, hopefully, the mom will be the one to do so.

Several months ago, my 18-year-old daughter and I were having a very warm (read "almost heated") discussion about her activities for the evening. Danna had plans that would obviously extend past her normal curfew and was pleading her case for leniency and a later time to be home. I was not sympathetic, because it was a school night. When we finally reached a compromise, her parting words were, "Mom, how about one more hour?" I was weakening, and she knew it, but with my last ounce of strength I responded, "I'll think about it." Smiling, she headed out the door.

When her curfew came and went, I called her cell phone, ready to wring her pretty little neck. "Hey, this is Danna. What's up, Mom?" she cheerfully answered, as if nothing were wrong. Clever girl! "What's up is that you are not home on time, which means you are grounded," I just as cheerfully responded. "Grounded? Mom, why am I grounded? You said you would think about it." Because I had not given a clear "no" she felt like she had grounds for dismissal of my case. Wrong—and consequences were meted out. However, I was reminded that silence can be interpreted to mean just about anything.

Confrontation is a gift we bring to every healthy relationship. We must also bring it to the unhealthy relationships with which we struggle. Confrontation is a spiritual surgery that tends to be painful. Without it, though, the cancer of contention and discord will remain intact, free to grow and spread its deadly relationship poison.

The Goal: Unity

The highest goal for every relationship is unity at some level. The apostle Paul was committed to unity and peace, no matter how impossible it might seem. It was a commitment rising out of the love he found in his personal relationship with God. Out of this love, Paul writes a letter to the church at Philippi, a church he had established. His heart and life were there, and his closest friends and deepest relationships were with the people of the Philippian church. It caused him great pain to discover the division among them, and he writes the letter as an encouragement to deal with and confront the ones causing the division. The letter is one of his personal corrections as well.

He describes the unity God expects to be exemplified in all relationships, the difficult ones as well as the easy ones. "Make my joy complete by being like-minded, having the same love, being one in spirit and purpose" (2:2). Impossible! It is impossible to meet these standards in every relationship. Being like-minded, having the same love, and being one in spirit and in purpose are the characteristics of deep, abiding relationships forged by time, shared experiences, and habitual choices. Exactly! God never calls us to be satisfied with anything less than these standards of excellence when it comes to the way we love each other. It is a calling that can only be realized through the power of God at work in our hearts. It requires a complete and total surrender of our personal agenda for every relationship we have...to God Himself.

Before Dan and I were married, I noticed several rough edges in his character that needed to be sanded away, and I felt like I was just the one for the job. After all, that's what wives are for—right? I decided to lie low for a few months, lulling him into a false sense of security while giving him a chance to make the changes on his own before I stepped in with my well-thought-out and, in my eyes at least, brilliant plan for his life. The only problem was, my plan didn't line up with his plan. In fact, he seemed oblivious to the character flaws that were blatantly obvious to me.

After a few months of marital bliss during which I was fine-tuning my "Fix Dan Plan," a seed of discontent took root and began to grow in my heart. The strength I had so admired in Dan now looked a whole lot like stubbornness. His ability to take a complicated issue, dissect it, and break it down into a three-step-plan now seemed patronizing and sometimes even meddlesome. What I had once embraced as his devotion to me now seemed like his need to control me. It was time for the execution of my sure-to-succeed plan of transforming my husband into the man God and I thought he should be.

It goes without saying that unity was the last thing on my mind or on my list of changes to be made. Looking back, I am certain I fit the bill of a sandpaper person deluxe at that point in Dan's life! But like most difficult people, I would not be deterred. The results were painfully disastrous.

Arguments over insignificant issues ensued as we battled each other for control of the relationship. Dan rebuffed each attack, confused and bewildered by the mysterious and not-so-wonderful change in his wife. Every area of our marriage suffered, and we were both miserable. Thankfully, my young but wise husband was committed to me, I was committed to him, and we were both committed to God and our marriage before Him. I will never forget the afternoon Dan confronted me in love and with amazing patience. I don't remember much of the conversation, but I do remember the words that broke my heart while saving our marriage: "Honey, I'm not sure what's going on between us. But I do know I want to love you like you need to be loved." There you have the recipe for a successful marriage as well as unity in relationships.

Instead of loving Dan how *he needed* to be loved I loved him like *I thought* he should be loved—with my requirements and my expectations, hoping he would have to do all of the changing while I did all of the controlling. I had a lot to learn about the art of confrontation—how it brings unity, peace, and joy to any relationship where it is invited to work.

Confrontation, Not Combat

Sandpaper people love a good fight and often mistake combat for confrontation. The two are not the same. Do not succumb to that misapprehension. Combat slowly erodes and splinters, while confrontation is a precision act that, when done correctly, improves and strengthens relationships. It is our responsibility to bring confrontation into the picture when dealing with sandpaper people. There is a right way and a wrong way to confront. The success of any confrontation depends upon understanding the difference between the two.

The apostle Paul had been in high places of authority and understood that in the business world, it was imperative for everyone involved to be on the same page, all working toward the same goal. I can only imagine his reaction to those believers in Philippi who didn't seem to understand or even value unity.

> My brothers, you whom I love and long for, my joy and crown...stand firm in the Lord, dear friends! I plead with Euodia and I plead with Syntyche to agree with each other in the Lord. Yes, and I ask you, loyal yokefellow, help these women who have contended at my side in the cause of the gospel, along with Clement and the rest of my fellow workers, whose names are in the book of life. Rejoice in the Lord always. I will say it again: Rejoice! (Philippians 4:1-4).

Paul's words make it clear he is serious about unity—serious enough to name names in front of the whole church: "I plead with Euodia and I plead with Syntyche to agree with each other in the Lord" (verse 2). When a body of believers received a letter in those days, it was read before the entire group. (No telephones or e-mail!) I can just see the culprits reddening in embarrassment at being reprimanded in front of everyone for their divisive behavior. *Euodia* actually meant "precious journey," while *Syntyche* meant "pleasant acquaintance." Obviously, these two women were not living up to their names.

When we lived in South Florida, Dan served as youth pastor and teaching pastor in two different churches. Many people knew who we were. In fact, we had to carefully choose the restaurant where we went for our weekly date in order to have time alone. We invariably ran into someone from church every time we went to the grocery store, gas station, local mall—you name it. It was a wonderful but sometimes difficult problem. We had to be "good" everywhere we went! We were living out every lesson we taught before the entire community. It was great accountability.

Unfortunately, a problem arose. We began receiving phone calls asking us to pay our bills. Dan had already paid them. Salesmen would call with some gadget Mr. Southerland had ordered. Dan never ordered anything over the phone. One day, after several months of trying to figure out what was going on, we received a notice from our credit-card company listing several charges we knew nothing about. Enough was enough. Detective Dan went into action and soon discovered that there were two Dan Southerlands living in the area. He remarked, "I need to call that man and tell him to either change his ways or change his name." I often wonder if God feels that way about those of us who call ourselves Christians. I am certain Paul felt that way about the two feuding women in the church at Philippi.

Euodia and Syntyche were not bad women and, in fact, had worked side by side with Paul. Evidently something happened. The Scripture doesn't say what issue caused the contention, which leads me to believe it was nothing important. It rarely is. Paul really doesn't seem to care what the problem was, he simply told them to fix it, to "agree with each other in the Lord." Paul isn't saying they must always agree or that there will never be another conflict between them. What Paul is telling them is to be agreeable in the Lord, to agree to disagree and then go on.

If You Love Someone, Level with Them

Remember that earlier in his letter to the church, Paul gave the requirements for being agreeable in the Lord—being like-minded, having the same love, being one in spirit and in purpose. These same requirements are also the basis for confrontation. The fact that we are called to confront *from* unity and love in order to *restore* unity and love confirms the truth that confrontation is a spiritual discipline of the mind, heart, will, and emotions. Too many times we allow undisciplined thinking and rash speaking to run rampant, leaving dissension in their wake. Paul would not allow it, and neither should we.

> If we are not careful, we will be drawn in to the world's system for resolving conflict. That system is called *retaliation*—it is from the pit, and it smells like smoke!

You may be asking yourself, *Why is it so important to guard unity in our relationships? What's the big deal?"* Jesus nails the answer to that question: "By this all men will know that you are my disciples, if you love one another" (John 13:35). In other words, our relationships prove there is a living God—by the way we love, by the way we forgive, and by the way we confront.

If we are not careful, we will be drawn into the world's system for resolving conflict. That system is called *retaliation*—it is from the pit, and it smells like smoke! God calls us, not to revenge or to retaliation, but to forgiveness and restoration. In fact, we are to pursue unity wholeheartedly, chasing after it and holding it firmly in our hearts: "Turn away from evil and do good. Try to live in peace even if you must run after it to catch and hold it!" (1 Peter 3:11 ICB).

If you love someone, you level with them. Being able and willing to confront in love is a mark of maturity and stability in the Christian life. "Then we will no longer be infants, tossed back and forth by the waves...instead, speaking the truth in love, we will in all things grow up into Him who is the Head, that is, Christ" (Ephesians 4:14). In our immaturity, we sometimes view confrontation as harmful and something to be avoided, hoping to take the easy way out of a sticky situation that needs to be dealt with. However, the book of the Bible that is chock-full of common sense, Proverbs, contradicts that thinking—"Faithful are the wounds of a friend" (27:6 NASB). The first time I read that verse, I thought it was just plain peculiar. Then I remembered we are called to be a "peculiar people," living in contradiction to the world's ways, walking in radical obedience, and adhering to seemingly paradoxical truths.

Honestly, God's ways sometimes make no sense to me. When I try to superimpose my human desire to avoid all pain on top of God's holy principle of confrontation, is simply doesn't fit. The truth is, confrontation hurts. Transformation is painful. Cutting away disease is usually agonizing. However, left unchecked, disease will grow out of control, affect every part of the body, and eventually bring death. It is only through God's redefinition of who we are and what we believe, that relationships can be what He intends them to be—healthy and joyful.

The "wound" referred to in Proverbs 27:6 is correction or confrontation for the good of a friend, someone we love. Pride and a preoccupation with self keep us from practicing confrontation. We avoid emotional discomfort. We want everyone to like us— admittedly, peace is much nicer than conflict. However, when we refuse to confront, we are placing our stamp of approval on a wrong action or attitude, one that needs confronting. Refusing to confront someone we love because it is difficult and uncomfortable for us is like holding their hand as they walk off a dangerous cliff. Refusing to confront sandpaper people can be just as dangerous. What are the keys to effective confrontation?

KEY 1: CONFRONT WITH THE RIGHT MOTIVE

Anyone who takes pleasure in confrontation is doing it with the wrong motive and for the wrong reason. The prerequisite for confrontation is daunting: "If someone is caught in a sin, *you who are spiritual* should restore him gently" (Galatians 6:1). We must examine our own lives before putting even one foot on the road to successful confrontation. We must be right with God before we can be right with others. Jesus is crystal-clear in His indictment of pride and arrogance as the motive for confrontation:

> In the same way you judge others, you will be judged, and with the measure you use, it will be measured to you. Why do you look at the speck of sawdust in your brother's eye and pay no attention to the plank in your own eye? How can you say to your brother, "Let me take the speck out of your eye," when all the time there is a plank in your own eye? You hypocrite, first take the plank out of your own eye, and then you will see clearly to remove the speck from your brother's eye (Matthew 7:2-6).

But when our hearts are right, our motives will be right. Winning is never the right motive. The right motive for confrontation is *always* restoration and "others"-oriented: "Do not let any unwholesome talk come out of your mouths, but only what is helpful for building others up according to their needs, that it may benefit those who listen" (Ephesians 4:29). In confrontation, we must always consider "their needs" before our own. Instead, we are often guilty of correcting or confronting someone in order to fulfill our need to express an emotion or bring about a desired change—*our* desired change.

When we choose to ignore our own flaws and failures, any confrontation we offer will be riddled with condemnation. Sandpaper people are mirrors. We often see in them what we don't want to see in ourselves, which means we must be willing to set aside our pride and our needs to attain the higher purpose of restoration. We first need to examine our heart motives for any trace of censure before speaking words of correction. When confronting your sandpaper person, check your heart motive.

KEY 2: CONFRONT IN THE RIGHT WAY

Paul encourages us to confront in the right way—gently. When we have just one nerve left (a badly frayed one) and our sandpaper person is romping on it, we tend to confront in anger, from pain and frustration, with little control. The explosion can be heard for miles around, and relationship debris is certain to fall. Healthy confrontation does not involve a weapon of any kind—verbal or nonverbal. We should speak honestly but gently. Confrontation wrapped in gentle love is powerful!

During our first years at Flamingo Road Church, Dan and I both struggled with maintaining a balanced schedule. It was so easy for him to work six or seven nights a week because the church was exploding in growth and a crisis was always at hand. Being the precious and loving wife that I am, I confronted Dan—*not* in love and *not* with gentleness. It did *not* work. I decided to back off and let God have a shot at him. The plan was to duck in order for God to deck Dan!

One afternoon while I was preparing dinner, the phone rang. It was Dan calling to say that one of the church members had just been admitted to the hospital with chest pains. Dan was planning to drop by the hospital, which meant he would be late for dinner and family night—again. He promised to make his visit short and be home as soon as possible. When Danna strolled through the kitchen checking out the dinner menu, she asked when her dad was coming home. I explained the situation but assured her that Dan would be home as soon as he could. She seemed satisfied with my explanation and headed for the family room. (Kids can be so sneaky!)

A few minutes later, I heard her talking to someone and stepped to the door of the family room. She was on the phone calling the church office. Her childlike but powerful words of confrontation stopped me in my tracks. "Dad, please come home. I don't like it when you have to work late. I know that man in the hospital needs you, but there are lots of doctors there. I only have one daddy and it makes me sad when you aren't here. I need to see you with my eyes." Dan came home, drawn by the loving and powerful confrontation of his daughter.

Every relationship in life improves with confrontation that's done the right way. In fact, the harder the truth, the more love we must use in sharing it, especially when it comes to sharing truth with sandpaper people. Here are some simple tips for effective confrontation:

- *Always begin with affirmation.* Encouraging words set the stage and prepare the heart to hear words of correction. Corrective words that fall on ears prepared by loving words are more likely to be heard and considered.

- *Be willing to take your part of the blame.* I have lived long enough to realize that no conflict is ever totally one-sided. Taking your share of the blame often defuses anger and steers the confrontation in the right direction.

- *Express hurt—not hostility.* It's important to keep emotions under control during confrontation. Volume negates listening. Raised voices and angry words slam the door shut on any good that might come from confrontation. Sandpaper people rarely realize the depth of the pain they inflict and may very well be surprised by what you are telling them. Express your feelings with words—not volume or accusation.

- *Make clear, direct statements.* When preparing for confrontation, I will often write down what I plan to say, then read it aloud—sometimes in front of the mirror. I can then go back and eliminate unnecessary comments, inflammatory words, or vengeful statements disguised as correction. In any confrontation, it is important to stick to the facts, refusing to become either hysterical or historical. Each confrontation is an entity unto itself and does not need to be lumped together with issues from the past.

- *Avoid using the words "never" and "always."* They are obviously untrue and accomplish little in a confrontation; they destroy the credibility of the person doing the confronting. These two words tend to stir up emotions and fan emotional fires.

- *Listen.* One of my favorite (but ineffective) tactics in confrontations is to use the time the other person is speaking to formulate my next point. As a result, I don't listen. I assume I already know what will be said. Difficult conversations require total attention. Listening validates people, while refusing to listen is arrogant and self-centered.

- *Be solution-centered.* It's all too easy to go for the "let's get this over with" conversation instead of the "let's get to the heart of this problem" discussion. Make the decision beforehand to stay at the table until a solution is found and restoration is achieved.

While the sandpaper people in your life are likely to be confronted on a regular basis, that confrontation usually comes from an unclean heart and an angry spirit. In fact, an inept confrontation can easily become just another chip on a sandpaper person's shoulder, giving them one more reason to be who they are—difficult. When love and gentleness deliver correction, it is much more likely to be received and acted on. We can be caring and confronting at the same time. Most sandpaper people are controllers and manipulators, intimidating their way into other people's lives, being what my kids would call "master control freaks." Sandpaper people mistakenly believe that manipulation is the only way they can gain entrance into lives. Confrontation is a spiritual exercise and an act of obedience to God that changes lives and builds healthy relationships.

KEY 3: CONFRONT AT THE RIGHT TIME

The only difference between a foul ball and a home run is timing. And when it comes to relationships, timing really is everything. Confrontation especially needs to be carried out at the right time. In Matthew 5:23 we find the clear directive to "go at once" and be reconciled with anyone who has offended us. In other words, the longer we wait, the harder it will usually be to arrive at a solution. When hurtful words and rash actions are allowed to sit, it is almost like they sprout and take root, making it more painful and more difficult for them to be removed.

My husband now travels full-time, training pastors to take their churches to a new level of reaching their communities for Christ. Neither Dan nor I like the fact we have to be apart several days a week—for many reasons. Traveling is exhausting. Add to that exhaustion the drain of teaching several hours a day and meeting with pastor after pastor for private consultations. Consequently, when he walks in the door, Dan is ready to collapse. I, on the other hand, have been at home all week, dealing with pets, housework, writing deadlines, speaking engagements, a teenage daughter who enjoys a very active social life, and running Journey Ministry. Consequently, I am ready to collapse before Dan collapses and, on top of that, I need to collapse while talking nonstop because I have so many things to tell him.

When Dan first started this new travel schedule, I would pick him up at the airport and on the way home, proceed to unload every problem I had faced all week—in a tone that implied, *If you were home, this would never have happened* or the ever-familiar *If you were home, you could have helped me deal with this issue.* One day, what I was doing hit me when Dan said, "I almost dread coming home." Since then, I have tried to give him some time for "re-entry" before bombarding him with the realities of life at home without him. Yes, he needs to hear everything I have to say. No, he doesn't have to hear it before even unpacking his bags. Timing is very important when it comes to tough conversations.

Admittedly, it is hard to rummage through the life of a difficult person in order to pinpoint a good time for confrontation. It is like walking across a minefield, wondering when you will lose some body part in an emotional explosion. Nevertheless, we must be committed to finding some time that is better than others to have that tough conversation with that tough person.

KEY 4: CONFRONT WITH THE RIGHT AUDIENCE

Learning to confront with the right audience is important in every relationship, but crucial when dealing with sandpaper people. The best way to confront is one-on-one, a key guideline that sandpaper people seem to delight in violating. If you are a parent, you are well-acquainted with a game children love to play, the "Mommy Is on the Phone and We Can Get Away with Murder" game. Sandpaper people often play the same game, deliberately choosing those moments when you are surrounded by people to do their finest work, hoping you won't explode in front of witnesses. Choose your audience carefully when confronting a difficult person.

Our son has played on many different football teams over the years. Every football player and every parent of a football player is familiar with the yelling that most football coaches occasionally use to gain the undivided attention of their players. One coach in particular was known for his abrasive behavior. After an especially grueling practice, one of Jered's teammates exploded in anger, furiously confronting this coach in front of the entire team. The situation escalated out of control, resulting in the young man walking off the field, refusing to play, and consequently being removed from the game roster. When I asked Jered for his interpretation of the incident, he responded, "Mom, I understand why Carl did what he did. He just chose the wrong place and the wrong way to do it. He should have gone by the coach's office and talked with him personally. He may not respect the coach, but he has to respect the position of coach." Jered went on to explain that had this young man handled the situation correctly, constructive change could have resulted. Instead, the player was alienated and the coach's behavior was unaffected. Confrontation done with the right audience can bring healthy change.

⌣⁀

Learning the art of confrontation is so important if we are to develop and cultivate relationships that please God and encourage others. But sometimes, even the best confrontation doesn't help. What then?

First, once again, adhere to the words of Paul: "If it is possible, as far as it depends on you, live at peace with everyone" (Romans 12:18). Some people refuse to accept any kind of confrontation and have no desire for peace or healing. Their pain has become their identity, and they are unwilling to relinquish it to gain peace or health. Even so, we still have a spiritual responsibility to that person and to God:

- *Check on them.* If you sense the hurt is still present or that you have been misunderstood, go back to that person and check on them. It may take them time to assimilate the conversation and work through their response.

- *Accompany that check with an act of love.* A note, a card, a small gift, a plate of homemade cookies, will sometimes seal the deal. It is a tangible way to stretch the confrontation to include one more dose of love.

- *Pray for that person.* Nothing changes attitudes and heals wounds like prayer. Before, during, and after confrontation, bathe that person in prayer, asking God to heal and restore them. Pray He will let you see them as He sees them. Ask for His love to work in you and through you in that person's life.

- *Give them a little time and space.* This step is sometimes hard for me because I want everything to be settled as quickly as possible. However, some people are slow processors and need extra time or space to process a confrontation. If you try to rush them, you will find yourself in the middle of another conflict as the result of your effort to control them and the situation. Let them go. Back off. Lay them at His feet and let Him work.

We were created to live in harmony and peace. Remember that God calls us to wage peace in every relationship. Part of winning the battle is learning to confront sandpaper people in the right way—God's way. Confrontation that is done in love will change lives, save relationships, and honor God.

SANDPAPER TIPS

Dirt stains on your shoes can be removed with the help of sandpaper or an emery board.[10]

A baseball scuffed with sandpaper will produce hard-to-hit throws. The "sandpaper ball" has become an illegal pitch.[11]

"Truing the tires." In just about any slot-car magazine, or any discussion on preparing a slot car for racing, you will come across this term. It refers to the process of making the tires round, or *true*.

Most slot cars that come straight off the shelf require some degree of truing of their wheels. One reason might be that the tires are simply out of round. Cars with out-of-round tires will tend to hop when up to speed, especially no-magnet or light-magnet cars. When the rear end starts hopping you will notice that cornering suffers the most, because the rear end is becoming light, even briefly airborne on one or more tires—and this causes the car to lose traction.

Another problem new cars have is not being flat against the track. Sometimes the centerline radius of the tire is less than the radius of the outer edge of the tire. This is referred to as *crowning*. The tire isn't utilizing as much of the tire surface as it could, and its traction will suffer on takeoff, braking, and cornering. Truing makes the tire flat.

To true a tire, use 150-grit sandpaper. Hold or tape it on the track, holding two free fingers on the controller hand. With your free hand, hold the car backwards on the track with the rear wheels over the sandpaper. Give the car full throttle, allowing the car to settle down onto the sandpaper, making sure that both wheels touch the track.[12]

Ten

Be Strong:
Develop Endurance

He gives strength to those who are tired
And more power to those who are weak.
Isaiah 40:29 NCV

SANDPAPER PEOPLE MAKE ME TIRED—literally. Dealing with difficult people drains my emotional energy and dulls my mental consistency. Exhaustion hovers over every interaction with them, while the spiritual questions arising from that interaction drive me to my knees. Like you, without the right kind of strength and enough of that strength, I'm doomed to failure in getting along with people who rub me the wrong way.

Strength is in great demand. Everywhere we look, gyms, fitness centers, and health clubs are popping up, all offering the "one and only" fitness program that will enable us to live the good life all the way to our hundredth birthday, with the looks of Catherine Zeta-Jones or Denzel Washington. Billboards and infomercials tell us to lift those weights, run that mile, stretch those muscles, and drink that shake. Kickboxing videos are flying off the shelves, while trainers are being hired as personal "Directors of Pain and Suffering." It seems as if we are determined to be healthy and strong.

Diet and exercise are good and right, but physical strength is not what I am after. I long for an *inner* strength that plays itself out in every relationship, making it possible to deal with and even embrace those people who constantly rub us the wrong way. Sandpaper people seem to sense any existing weakness and then use it to their advantage. Our slightest wavering in emotional stability is their signal for action.

Sandpaper children are pros at this maneuver. Max Lucado tells a story about his youngest daughter, who knew her daddy was wrapped securely around her little finger. Most of the time she could get whatever she wanted from him as long as it was not extravagant or harmful—until the day of the new bicycle. The youngster was very upset because her older sister was getting a new bike—one without training wheels. She wanted one too. Her dad explained that her sister was older, bigger, and more experienced. The little girl still wanted a new bike. She cried, pleaded, bargained, and even pouted, but nothing changed her dad's mind. Finally, in frustration, Lucado looked at his daughter and said, "I know you don't understand, but this time you will have to trust your dad to make the right decision." His youngest child thought for a minute, then said, "No! I'll just need to get me a new daddy!" That is exactly the thinking of many sandpaper people. They aim for the weakest spot, and when it doesn't give way, they simply move on to a new target. It takes strength to withstand the emotional attacks and maneuvers of sandpaper people.

Relationships with sandpaper people are depleting, consuming "emotional black holes" that are capable of draining every ounce of energy we possess. If we are not careful, the difficult relationships will bring about our emotional bankruptcy.

A Strong Example

Queen Esther was a woman whose life models the kind of strength we need in dealing with difficult people. Haman was

King Ahasuerus' right-hand man and hated all Jews, Esther and Esther's cousin Mordecai in particular. Out of his hatred came a plan that would persuade the king to pass a law demanding that all people must bow to the king or die! Knowing the strong faith of the Jewish people, Haman was certain they would refuse to bend a knee to anyone but God. When Esther heard of the plot, she was terrified because she was a Jew, a fact she had neglected to tell her husband, the king. Haman's law would mean her death as well as the death of her nation.

Anticipating their doom, Esther and her people fasted and prayed for God's direction and protection. Then she did what many clever women do when faced with a crisis. She threw a dinner party and followed it with a second one, during which she revealed Haman's villainous plot along with the juicy little tidbit that she was indeed a Jew. Furious, Ahasueras condemned Haman to die, and the Jewish nation was saved through the faith and strength of the queen.

In examining the life of Esther, we see the strength and confidence with which she handled the biggest crisis of her life and the grittiest sandpaper person she had ever encountered. Though at first glance she seems to be a woman of great strength, in reality she was terrified and weak, her heart flawed with human shortcomings—just like us. Her weakness was the perfect setting for a miracle because, as Paul writes, God's best work is transforming weakness into strength: "My power works best in your weakness" (2 Corinthians 12:9). In dealing with people who rub us the wrong way, we need to embrace the truth that while our strength is inadequate, God's strength is more than enough.

A little girl listened attentively as her father read a passage from the Bible. Every night, her mom and dad talked about God, describing the miracle of His love and power. She had been thinking about Him but had a question. Placing her little hands on her daddy's knees, the little girl gazed into his eyes and asked, "Daddy, how big is God?" Her father thought for a moment before answering. "Honey, he is always just a little bigger than you need."

It is that "bigger strength" we must rely upon in every difficult relationship.

God is waiting to unleash His power—waiting on our invitation and permission to work. We give that invitation for His strength and power to attend us in the form of choices we make. Relationships are riddled with choices. Every word, each attitude and action, is a choice in the relationship structure. The strength and stability of the foundation depends upon our choices. The tougher the relationship, the tougher the choices; tough, but not impossible, if each choice is made in and through the power of God.

I have a love–hate relationship with a passage of Scripture that clearly lays out the choices we must make. I find this passage to be extremely important, not only to living a life of victory but to the success of any relationship in life as well.

> Be humble under God's powerful hand so he will lift you up when the right time comes. Give all your worries to him, because he cares about you. Control yourselves and be careful! The devil, your enemy, goes around like a roaring lion looking for someone to eat. Refuse to give in to him, by standing strong in your faith. You know that your Christian family all over the world is having the same kinds of suffering. And after you suffer for a short time, God, who gives all grace, will make everything right. He will make you strong and support you and keep you from falling. He called you to share in his glory in Christ, a glory that will continue forever (1 Peter 5:6-10 NCV).

Choices are habit makers and bondage breakers. It is the word chosen, the attitude preferred, and the action selected that invite God to work—choices that invite Him to permeate every part of a relationship with His persistent love and regenerating power. All that is required of us is to choose.

CHOICE 1: CHOOSE HUMILITY OVER PRIDE

Be humble under God's powerful hand so he will lift
you up when the right time comes (1 Peter 5:6 NCV).

Humility is painful at times but is powerful at all times.
Humility chooses total abandonment, a complete submission to
God. Esther was humble, understanding the power of submission
as she willingly submitted to her cousin and her husband, as well
as to God and His very confusing plan for her life. To me, Esther's
self-abandoning trust in God is her strongest quality. Can you
imagine the thoughts that must have camped out in her mind?
*You want me to be a queen? I am only a kid, God, a teenager! I've
got other plans! I have no idea how to be a queen! You definitely need
to get someone else for this job!* Yet this fearful young woman laid
aside every doubt, tabled every question, and walked through her
fear, following a plan that made absolutely no sense to her and, I
am sure, seemed certain to end in failure. She trusted God. The
result was far beyond anything she could have dreamed possible,
as Mordecai observed: "You may have been chosen queen for just
such a time as this" (Esther 4:14 NCV).

When we choose humility over pride, we acknowledge the
power of God and give Him permission to transform every difficult relationship into a showcase for His transforming love. Even
the most difficult person cannot override our choice of humility
over pride.

CHOICE 2: CHOOSE PEACE OVER WORRY!

Give all your worries to him, because he cares about
you (1 Peter 5:7 NCV).

My husband often says there are two kinds of people in the
world—those who have ulcers and those who give them. Sandpaper people are definitely ulcer-giving people, unless we learn to
choose peace over worry. Getting along with people who rub you
the wrong way is difficult at best and can sometimes make peace

seem impossible to find. But that is only true if peace is dependent on outer circumstances and relationships. It isn't, though. Peace is an inside job and comes only from God. Nothing can take the place of peace, nor can it be counterfeited.

Sandpaper people are not peaceful people. One of the reasons they are rough around the edges is because they are not at rest—with God, with themselves, or with others. They may not know God—or if they do, they are ignorant of who they are in Him and who He wants to be in their lives. Sandpaper people continually arrange the circumstances of their lives in order to set themselves up for failure, proving to everyone, including God and even their own heart, that what everyone believes about them is true—they are worthless. We must not be fooled by their temper tantrums, boisterous antics, or brooding silences. These are all traps of their own making that sooner or later will imprison them in disappointment and defeat. Worry is their jailor. Worry is a control issue. It is playing God, foolishly thinking we can handle difficult relationships on our own. Every time we choose to worry, we are choosing not to trust, as this verse explains— "You, LORD, give true peace to those who depend on you, because they trust you" (Isaiah 26:3 NCV).

Have you ever noticed that, for people who rub you the wrong way, everything is a big deal? Drama, even hysteria, flows freely through the veins of every sandpaper person I have ever met. Under the spotlight of opportunity, everything, no matter how insignificant it may seem, escalates into a major crisis filled with worry, distorting what is real. But in 1 Peter 5:7, as we saw on the previous page, we discover that the secret of handling worry is casting every care on Him. I love this verse because, in essence, it is saying that God has volunteered to be the dumping ground for every fear, every worry, and every sandpaper person. We need to daily, minute by minute, take those difficult people to God and leave them there, in the palm of His hand. Oh, yes—I know they will come crawling back, but stand firm in your resolve to keep taking them back to the place of wholeness.

Esther was confronted with a frightening set of circumstances. By human standards she had every right to worry. Taken from her home, she was thrust into the daunting role of queen and given the overwhelming responsibility for an entire nation's future—if she escaped death at Haman's hand. Talk about the perfect chance to work up a huge mountain of worry! Instead, Esther chose to trust God. She fasted, prayed, and trusted. The result was a solution to her problem and a peace in her heart.

> hen we live in peace, we are paving the way for difficult people to encounter Peace Himself.

We sometimes miss the solution to handling our sandpaper person because we allow worry to take us hostage. In British Columbia, Canada, stood an old penitentiary. When it was being torn down, the workmen made an interesting discovery. The gates were made of steel and the windows were covered with iron bars. However, the outer walls were made of wood covered with clay and paper, painted to look as if they were thick stone. Anyone could have easily gone through those walls, but no one ever tried.

Sandpaper people remain sandpaper people because fear keeps us from stepping out in faith to help and love them. We are afraid of their reaction or lack of reaction. We are afraid of what others will think. We are afraid we will be sucked into a relationship we really don't want, a relationship with no exit door. However, we need to prefer others over self, faith over fear. The apostle Paul instructs us to choose peace and "not worry about anything. But pray and ask God for everything you need. And when you pray, always give thanks. And God's peace will keep your hearts and minds in Christ Jesus. The peace that God gives is so great that we cannot understand it" (Philippians 4:6-7 NCV).

Since peace is foreign to the sandpaper person, someone else's life of peace can shock this often turbulent type into seeing the very thing for which they long—the peace of God. When we live in peace, we are paving the way for difficult people to encounter Peace Himself. Choose peace over worry!

CHOICE 3: CHOOSE KNOWLEDGE OVER IGNORANCE!

> Control yourselves and be careful! The devil, your enemy, goes around like a roaring lion looking for someone to eat. Refuse to give in to him, by standing strong in your faith. You know that your Christian family all over the world is having the same kinds of suffering (1 Peter 5:8-9 NCV).

Spiritual ignorance is not bliss—it's dangerous. Many people say it doesn't really matter what you believe as long as you believe something. I totally disagree! The apostle Paul writes in 1 Thessalonians 5:21-22, "Test everything. Hold on to the good. Avoid every kind of evil." In order to deal with sandpaper people, we must be able to discern between truth and lies.

If the enemy can dupe us into believing his lies, those difficult relationships will eventually damage and even destroy our emotional health, seeping into the broken places, ripping open almost healed wounds. Complete honesty must guide every difficult relationship because sandpaper people must always be confronted with sound, solid truth exhibited in clear and transparent conversation as well as disciplined behavior. We are in a battle for godly relationships. In order to win that battle we must take action!

Identify the Enemy

> The devil, your enemy, goes around like a roaring lion looking for someone to eat (1 Peter 5:8 NCV).

Sandpaper people are not the enemy. It is sometimes easier to convince ourselves that they are, as it would make the attack plan so much simpler and less guilt-inducing. We could simply do everything in our power to eliminate those people from our lives. But what God really wants is for us to embrace them, celebrating the truth that where they are is no surprise to Him. Esther's enemy was not only Haman, but evil working through Haman, a very important distinction. Satan would love to foster any attack on sandpaper people, encouraging us to ignore the hand of God in the matter.

When our children were in middle school, some of their friends received laser guns for Christmas. One weekend, they brought the guns to our house for a "big, bad laser war." The kids divided into teams—the object of the game was simple, to wipe out the enemy. Wonderful! What clean, wholesome fun! Hours went by to the sound of war whoops, shouts and threats, and cries of victory. They had a great time playing with those guns— until it was dark. I stood in the kitchen preparing dinner, when I heard the kitchen door open and close—uh, *slam*—and looked up to see Danna, red-faced with fury. I knew it would not be long before I had every morbid detail of whatever injustice she had endured at the hand of "those boys."

I was right. "Mom, I need to talk to you—now!" I knew a command when I heard it, so I dropped my spatula and waited for the story. It was short and not so sweet. "Everybody is mad at me because I keep shooting my own team." So far, I was totally lost. I guess my confusion was evident because I could sense the exasperation that fueled her next words. "Mom! Are you listening?" I was—it didn't help. With a sigh and in her most patronizing tone, my daughter explained, "I keep shooting my own team. It's so dark I can't tell who the enemy is." We often assign sandpaper people the role of "enemy," when they are not our adversary but rather, our mission field.

Getting along with people who rub us the wrong way is dependent on understanding that Satan is at work around us, encouraging us to take up weapons of strife, anger, frustration and misunderstanding. Victory is ours, though, unless we hand it over to the enemy. So ignoring him is foolish, but if we identify him and expose his malignant tactics, we deprive him of power and negate his ability to control and manipulate relationships.

Use the Right Weapon

> Refuse to give in to him, by standing strong in your faith (1 Peter 5:9 NCV).

In any battle, the wrong choice of weapons can be fatal. That is especially true when trying to get along with difficult people. It is imperative that we choose the right weapon. Peter could have listed many weapons, but he names only one—faith. Faith honors God, and God honors faith. "Without faith it is impossible to please God" (Hebrews 11:6).

The shield in a Roman soldier's wardrobe was wooden, about three feet wide and four feet tall, and overlaid with leather to deflect arrows tipped with fire. The shield protected every other piece of armor, which is why in Ephesians 6:16 Paul instructs us to "take up the shield of faith." Faith is our shield of protection in every part of our spiritual walk; it is the covering for every healthy relationship. By feeding our faith in God, we are laying a foundation of supernatural inner strength that will equip and enable us to interact with sandpaper people in the way Jesus would. I like the Chinese tale of an old man describing his inner conflict: "It is like two dogs fighting. One is good and one is evil. They fight constantly for the control of my life!" When asked which one would win, the old man replied, "The one I feed the most." The more we feed our faith, the stronger it grows! Satan hates faith because it stops him dead in his tracks! However, misplaced faith is powerless. When it comes to dealing with sandpaper people, we must be careful not to place faith in our own human ability to handle that relationship.

Misplacing faith is just as dangerous as having no faith. A newspaper story told of a Midwestern hospital where officials discovered that the firefighting equipment had not been properly installed. For 35 years, hundreds of medical staff and thousands of patients strongly believed in and trusted this system, but it had never been attached to the city's water main. The pipe from the building extended four feet underground—and then stopped! The expensive equipment was adequate for the building—but it was useless because it lacked the most important thing—water! Their faith was real, but it was dangerously misplaced! Ignorance about faith, a misplaced faith, or the absence of faith hollows out footholds for the enemy, inviting ruin.

Esther's faith was in the right place—in God. It was strong, even though she was frightened by the thought of facing Haman and the destruction of the Jewish nation, as well as the loss of her own life. But she chose to walk by that faith, not by sight. Faith yanks the question marks of life into exclamation points and is a mighty weapon in the battle for godly relationships.

CHOICE 4: CHOOSE CHARACTER OVER COMFORT

> After you suffer for a short time, God, who gives all grace, will make everything right. He will make you strong and support you and keep you from falling. He called you to share in his glory in Christ, a glory that will continue forever (1 Peter 5:10 NCV).

Over the years, our son has endured several football injuries, but as a junior in high school, Jered experienced his first surgery, in order to repair a broken bone in his foot (the fifth metatarsal, to be exact). The surgeon explained exactly what he would do. "First of all, I will remove the scar tissue that has formed around the break. I will then insert a metal screw to connect the broken bones." As he spoke, I was comforted by my mind's depiction of a shiny, thin, and smooth metal screw resting gently in my son's foot. There are times when ignorance is a blessing.

The surgery went well, and after two weeks, I took Jered in for a follow-up visit, during which the doctor x-rayed his foot to make sure it was healing properly. The smiling doctor walked in, waving an X-ray in his hand. "Your foot is healing beautifully," he announced with great pride. Curious, I asked the doctor if we could see. As he slapped the film up against the light box, I was horrified to see a long, thick screw. In fact, on closer examination, I was certain I could see the beginnings of rust on that barbaric instrument of torture jammed up into my son's precious bone.

Seeing the look on my face, the doctor assured me everything was fine. I was far from convinced and had a few questions that needed answering—immediately. "Is that screw supposed to look like that, or did you put the wrong screw in his foot? Will he be able to play football? Will that screw hurt when it rains? Will we now have to leave an hour earlier in order to catch a flight because that enormous screw will set off airport security detectors? Will the foot be as strong as it was before the surgery?" The doctor listened patiently and said, "Well, now that you mention it, I need to be honest and tell you it will not be as strong as it was before." He then grinned wickedly. "It will actually be stronger." Jered is now in college and has just had knee surgery for a torn ligament. Again, my questions were "Will he be able to play football on this knee? Will it be as strong as it was before the injury?" Once again, a surgeon smiled and assured me that the knee would be stronger than it was before. I find it interesting that all through life, the greatest strength is forged in the broken places. The same is true in dealing with difficult people.

God is not committed to our comfort. God is committed to creating His character within us. One way He does that is through the abrasive and coarse work of sandpaper people as they grind off and sand away those rough edges, even to the point of breaking. Suffering comes in many ways, but always with the purpose of making us strong enough to endure pain and weak enough to rely upon God.

Many times, difficult relationships cause the most pain. Peter writes that God will "make everything right," which indicates that God's promises take our circumstances and relationships, adjust them, and make the broken pieces fit together in order to equip us for service. "Making everything right" can also be translated from the original language as "mending nets." A fisherman's net was a vital part of his livelihood. A broken net meant no fish. One broken net affected the fisherman's ability to make a living and provide for his family. Therefore, it was imperative for the fisherman to keep his nets in working condition, constantly mending the broken places.

Every time we are broken but allow God to do the mending, new strength comes. Paul, certainly no stranger to trials, pain, and broken nets, declared. "We know that these troubles produce patience. And patience produces character, and character produces hope" (Romans 5:3-4 NCV). I must admit, I have been known to insert the name of my current sandpaper person into that verse so that it reads, for example, "I know that *Jack* produces patience. And patience produces character, and character produces hope." What an amazing progression—from a difficult relationship to godly character and then on to hope! Hope follows pain because it is in pain we are forced to trust God and His power to mend a broken life. The difficult relationships in life and the brokenness they bring will make us bitter or better. It is our choice. We can insist on comfort and forfeit character, or we can embrace the brokenness, knowing that God will use it to make us strong.

Sandpaper people are grindstones. Whether they grind us down or polish us up depends on what we are made of. Harry Truman said, "Fame is a vapor, popularity is an accident, riches take wings, those who cheer today may curse tomorrow, and only one thing endures—character."

I believe sandpaper people, deep down, pray the silent prayer that someone will be strong enough to stop their vicious cycle of offensive behavior before it leads to the destruction of something or someone. I also believe that God allows difficult relationships to come into our daily walk in order to strengthen us for that very task.

SANDPAPER UTILIZATION

Sanding is necessary drudge work, improved only by spending less time doing it. You can't go right buying cheap sandpaper, but it's still easy to go wrong with the best sandpaper that's available. The key to choosing the right sandpaper is to know how the many different kinds of sandpaper work. Each component, not just the grit, contributes to the sandpaper's performance, determining how quickly it works, how long it lasts, and how smooth the results will be. If you know how the components work together, you'll be able to choose your sandpaper wisely and use it efficiently. Then you won't waste time sanding or end up burning the project in your fireplace.

For best results…

- Always use the correct type and grade of sandpaper for the job at hand—do not use paper sold for "hand sanding" in a power tool.

- Start by using a medium- or coarse-grade paper. Change the grade of paper you are using as the job progresses.

- Let the abrasive grit do the work; do not use undue pressure, because it will only clog the paper or cause it to wear out too quickly. When power-sanding, very little pressure is necessary—just guiding the tool is normally sufficient.

- Use a sanding block when hand-sanding.

- Move sandpaper *along* the grain of bare timber, not across.

- On a smooth, nongrained surface, move the sandpaper in small circular motions.

- Store sandpapers carefully in a cool dry area. Except for papers made using waterproof adhesive and backing material, any dampness may cause the adhesive or backing to fail or weaken, and grains will become detached.

- If the paper becomes clogged after a short time of use, look at the surface being sanded; if it is timber, the timber may be damp—allow time for it to dry. [13]

Be Thankful:
Thank God for Them

No matter what happens, always be thankful,
for this is God's will for you who belong to Christ Jesus.
Philippians 4:6 NLT

I HAVE A FRIEND WHO HAS TAUGHT fourth grade Bible in a Christian school for more than 20 years. In an effort to help her students understand that Thanksgiving is not only a national celebration but also should be a way of living and a heart attitude, she assigned her students the task of writing a report concerning the holiday's origins. Self-control is of course one of the most important qualities in a good teacher, but one report in particular had my friend close to hysterical laughter. Here's how it began:

> The pilgrims came here seeking freedom of "you-know-what." When they landed, they gave thanks to "you-know-who." Because of them, we can worship on Sunday "you-know-where."

Though we laugh at this child's leaving God's name out of his report, in fact, many of us are guilty of leaving Him out of our lives. We have given our heart to Him but, somewhere along the way, we have taken it back, one piece at a time. A cherished sin, an ungodly attitude, one wrong choice leading to other wrong choices—and selfish gain is once again seated on the throne of our hearts. When we leave God out of life's daily equation, there will be no attitude of thankfulness or gratitude because our natural "self," by its very nature, is never satisfied. It always craves something more to fill the emptiness and longing that a life without God creates.

Learning to live in thanksgiving gear is a life-changing discipline that will revolutionize the perspective with which we view both life and eternity. Giving thanks should be a natural characteristic of and a mark of maturity in the life of every believer. Being thankful is the acknowledgment of all God has done, as well as all He is going to do. Our choice to be thankful creates an awareness of His presence that, in turn, produces more thanksgiving.

An Opportunity to Be Thankful

With sandpaper people, learning to be thankful is one of the most important choices we *can* make as well as one of the most difficult choices we *must* make in order to bring any measure of health to those relationships. It's hard to be thankful when an abrasive person is in our face and breaking our heart. Their behavior may create harsh conflict and emotional outbursts that undermine our self-control. At times, we cannot see, hear, or understand what God is doing through difficult relationships or how He can possibly be at work in them. Therefore, we must, in faith, choose our response before the emotional confusion and mental chaos of difficult relationships erupts.

In Philippians 4:6, Paul puts forth a seemingly impossible command to be thankful no matter what happens and for one reason only—because it's God's will. Being thankful is obedience to God and the key to a life perspective of gratitude.

My husband has been in ministry for almost 30 years. While working with people is sometimes messy and not meant for the fainthearted, Dan and I have been on staff at several amazing churches. We have been loved, supported, and followed by the people God has allowed us to serve. I can honestly say that every church experience has been incredible, except one—the first one.

While attending seminary, Dan was the youth pastor of a small church that seemed to be teetering on the edge of explosive growth. A gifted pastor and talented worship leader stood in the pulpit. The people were loving, encouraging, and down-to-earth. It seemed like the perfect place to build a dynamic youth ministry—which is exactly what God did. We formed a youth choir, which grew explosively and was soon spilling out of the choir loft each time they sang. Dan began teaching to relevant issues the youth faced every day, challenging them to stand for Christ even when they had to stand alone. In a church of just over 300 attendees, we had more than 100 youth each week. It was a "God-thing," and it was very exciting…until the Sunday Dan preached his first sermon.

My husband is a master teacher, a student of the Word and lover of God's truth. As part of "Youth Sunday," Dan was asked to fill the pulpit. Afterward, people filled the aisles of that small sanctuary to hug and encourage him. Compliments flowed freely, and the common theme seemed to be "You need to teach more!" Little did we know that Dan's message was the beginning of the end for us at that church. In fact, one of the deacons shook Dan's hand and said, "Son, you need to pack your bags. You won't be here long." Dan and I took his words as an encouragement. They were meant, however, to be a warning.

It was only months later that Dan slipped a farewell letter under the door of the pastor's study and walked away from one of his most exciting times in ministry. The details are ugly and not worth mentioning, but the end result certainly is. Dan could have easily split that church by simply telling the truth. However, he chose a higher path when, with grace and integrity, he chose to forgive the pastor and people involved in forcing his resignation. Personally, I wanted to put out a contract on them, but thankfully, I had a committed husband, who simply wanted to do God's will. Looking back, we both thank God for that horrific circumstance because it broke us and taught us to trust and thank Him, no matter what. We learned that He is always enough and that His will penalizes no one. We knew without a doubt He had called us to that church, which meant that He was neither caught off guard nor unaware of the difficult circumstances that brought us to our knees.

Since that painful beginning, God has blessed every church Dan has served. Today, as I mentioned earlier, God is using him to train pastors across the world in changing their churches to effectively reach the communities around them for Christ. His book *Transitioning: Leading Your Church Through Change* has sold more than 50,000 copies in English and has, so far, been translated into eight languages. Dan has led more than 200 conferences for pastors and church leaders. I share those details not to brag on Dan but because I am certain that one of the reasons God is using Dan is due to the way he responded to the trial of that first church experience. We didn't understand why it happened, but we knew God did—and that was all that mattered. He took a handful of sandpaper people and used them to purify our hearts and clarify His calling in our lives. When we are tempted to doubt His hand of purpose or the certainty of His provision, we recall with gratitude that trial by fire and the lessons we learned.

A Choice for Thanks

Lives under the control of God will be characterized by joy and thanksgiving, even when we're trying to get along with sandpaper people. In Proverbs 10:28 we find the truth that "the prospect of the righteous is joy." The word "prospect" means *view* or *anticipation*. The "righteous" mentioned in this verse refer to those who have been made righteous or given right standing through a personal relationship with Him. He is Boss. He is Lord. When Jesus comes into our lives, He comes bringing joy, ready to spread it throughout our lives and deposit it into our very souls. God alone can produce joy and make it a living reality because, by definition, joy is the inner confidence He is in control.

And giving thanks is joy in action. To be joyful is to be thankful. It is important to remember that nowhere in this passage does Paul tell us we have to *feel* thankful. What he does say is that God commands us to *be* thankful always and in every situation. With difficult people, our first and foremost heart attitude should be thankfulness, and our first step of action should be to thank God for their presence in our lives. To do so is a step of faith initiated by an attitude of trust. Friends merely push us to *reach* our potential, while sandpaper people push us *beyond* it, all the way to brokenness.

One day a Bible student came across Deuteronomy 6:6: "These commandments that I give you today are to be upon your hearts." He didn't understand the verse and asked his teacher, "Why does it say to put the commandments of God *upon* our hearts and not *in* our hearts?" The teacher wisely responded, "It is not within man's power to place truth directly in his heart. All we can do is to place them on the surface of the heart, so that when the heart breaks, they fall in!"

Right now, thank God for your sandpaper person. Thank Him for every time that difficult relationship has left you wounded and bleeding. Thank Him for the inner strength that has been cultivated at the hands of every difficult person in your life. Thank Him for the spiritual discipline that is now your hedge of protection, and that it has come as the result of practicing self-control in abrasive relationships. It is through the broken places that the promises of God fall into our hearts, producing His character and nature in us.

God is drawn to broken people. When a difficult relationship has shattered every dream and destroyed all human hope, His love is enough. It is in a thankful heart that He resides. It is in our praises that He is at home: "You are holy, enthroned in the praises of Israel" (Psalm 22:3 NKJV). It is amazing to think that we can enthrone God in every situation and every relationship by praising Him. Thankfulness transforms our everyday surroundings and difficult relationships into a dwelling place for Him; and where He dwells there is more than enough power, strength, and victory to meet the demands of getting along with people who rub us the wrong way.

Praise and thankfulness are powerful and can set us free from the burdens we often bear alone and in our own strength. However, to sandpaper people, praise and thanksgiving are foreign languages. Their native tongue seems to be criticism and displeasure. Because there is no contentment, there can be no gratitude. They are often incapable of understanding genuine gratitude as well as quite incapable of choosing to be thankful for anyone or anything. As a result, dissatisfaction and unhappiness reign in and ultimately spill out of their hearts in a flood, carrying anger, frustration, and even fear. They may try to divert that tumult of emotions into a hidden channel, but it will still seep out in the form of rude behavior,

> They're all good days. It's what we put in them that will change them. When we "put" thanksgiving into a relationship, that relationship will change.

annoying traits, or caustic words. When we choose to be thankful, standing firm in the truth that praise and thanks are the dwelling place of God Himself, our response to that sandpaper person may very well change their life and ours as well. Being thankful and choosing praise is powerful—for many reasons.

A pastor tells of a beautiful lesson he learned one day when he casually wished one of his older church members a good day. The man remarked, "They're all good days. It's what we put in them that will change them." When we "put" thanksgiving into a relationship, that relationship will change. I suspect that being thankful for a sandpaper person may very well be one of the most powerful steps we can take in allowing God to work through us to transform him or her into a velvet person.

The apostle Paul was a master at inserting joy and thanksgiving into the most difficult relationships and the most complicated situations. A profound but straightforward man who understood and experienced joy in its truest sense, he wrote his letter to the church at Philippi in the midst of circumstances that would seem to produce anything but thankfulness.

Paul was in prison, alone and abandoned by man, awaiting his trial, facing almost certain death. This loyal disciple had been persecuted, beaten, stoned, and ridiculed because of his faith in God. His health was poor and he was apparently almost blind. He had no earthly reason to be thankful. Gratitude is not an earthly treasure, but rather a heavenly gift from God, who is committed to the joy of His children.

The story of the little girl who misquoted her favorite Bible verse, John 3:16, offers a clear picture of the verse's true meaning: "...that whosoever believeth in him should not perish, but have ever-laughing life." Jesus came, not just to give us life but to give us a life of joy, a life of sheer abundance in every sense of the word.

God not only wants us to experience joy, but He wants us to give away the joy we have received. That's where sandpaper people come in. Every sandpaper person is in desperate need of joy. When we choose to be thankful for that difficult person, we are making a deposit of joy in their life. Being thankful is a powerful choice we should make, for several reasons.

REASON 1: BEING THANKFUL BRINGS GOD PLEASURE

> Give thanks in all circumstances, for this is God's will
> for you in Christ Jesus (1 Thessalonians 5:18).

Nothing pleases the heart of a father like the obedience of his child. To thank and praise God is to obey Him. Praise is not a feeling, but the result of a life wholly surrendered to God. God seeks people who truly worship and praise Him, because it is His will. When we do His will, He is pleased. "If you love me, you will obey what I command" (John 14:15). Praise brings God pleasure.

REASON 2: BEING THANKFUL DEEPENS OUR TRUST

> Then will I go to the altar of God, to God, my joy and
> my delight. I will praise you with the harp, O God, my
> God (Psalm 43:4).

When we practice praise, trials become faith-builders, and difficult relationships become instruments of growth. Thankfulness helps us measure our problems against His limitless power, turning stumbling blocks into stepping-stones.

REASON 3: BEING THANKFUL FREES US FROM HAVING TO UNDERSTAND OUR CIRCUMSTANCES

> He who sacrifices thank offerings honors me and he prepares the way so that I may show him the salvation of God (Psalm 50:23).

I once heard Chuck Swindoll say, "The sovereignty of God is the Christian's security blanket." What a beautiful picture of God's dominion! When we understand that God really is in control, everything changes. We can face the questions of tomorrow and the shadows of yesterday. The future is filled with possibilities and the hope of heaven itself. Our soul is at rest and each step filled with joy when we stand on the truth that God is not only able and willing to work, but already is at work through our difficult relationships. Thanking and praising God in every circumstance solidifies faith and shatters doubt.

I can be a control freak, always demanding to know "why" and constantly badgering God for an explanation or a tally of my current situation. "I don't understand why this difficult relationship persists. I don't like the fact that sandpaper people keep popping up in my journey. Abrasive people irritate me and drive me to the brink of..." Ah, yes. Brinks are great places to encounter God and practice praise and thankfulness. They eliminate my need to understand my circumstances because I know they are in His hands, not mine.

REASON 4: BEING THANKFUL TRANSFORMS TRAGEDY INTO TRIUMPH

> These [trials] have come so that your faith—of greater worth than gold, which perishes even though refined

by fire—may be proved genuine and may result in praise, glory and honor when Jesus Christ is revealed (1 Peter 1:7).

I am told that in the famous lace shops of Belgium, there are certain rooms used for spinning the finest and most delicate designs of lace. Each room is completely dark—except for one small window. Through this tiny window, light shines directly on the work at hand. A solitary spinner works in the darkness, sitting where the narrow stream of light will fall on the delicate thread. The choicest pieces of lace, the most exquisite designs, are created when the worker is in the dark and only his work is in the light. With sandpaper people, we often find ourselves sitting in the darkness of frustration and pain, wondering if anything good can be salvaged from that painful relationship.

I will never forget the day I learned that God really can turn broken into beautiful. I was sitting at my desk, working on an assignment from my counselor. For months, I had been wrestling with my past; slowly, methodically working through painful issues and buried memories that seemed to be feeding the clinical depression I was battling. As page after page filled with harsh realities, a memory slammed into my heart and mind.

The pain was overwhelming as a vile scene from my childhood slowly took shape. I could hardly breathe as I frantically tried to escape the certainty I had been molested. The perpetrator had been our family doctor and friend. He had even provided free medical treatment when we had no money to pay. I had trusted him, counted on him. As a nurse, my mother had worked beside this man every single day and often watched his children when he and his wife were out of town.

Anger unlike any I had ever known fueled violent thoughts of revenge and retaliation. I was angry with this man—and angry with God. How could He have let this happen? Where was the light in this dark place?

For months, I worked through painful memories and raging emotions until I saw the first glimmer of light. It was wrapped in chosen forgiveness. And I began to see that had I never been wounded so badly, I would never have been able to forgive so freely—and in doing so, discover a depth of healing and freedom only the greatest pain can produce. Today, I can honestly thank God for all He has accomplished in me through the sin of that sandpaper person.

There are no accidents with God, nor is He surprised by anything or anyone in the life of His child. God uses even the most horrendous circumstances for our good. The same can be said of relationships. Every relationship—difficult or easy—comes to us for a purpose, wrapped in God's love and plan and faithfully delivered with His permission! The apostle Paul gives clear directions for the handling of these difficult relationships: "Live in peace with each other. Encourage the timid, help the weak, be patient with everyone. Make sure that nobody pays back wrong for wrong, but always try to be kind to each other and to everyone else. Be joyful always; pray continually; give thanks in all circumstances, for this is God's will for you in Christ Jesus" (1 Thessalonians 5:13-18). It is only in God's economy that being thankful transforms tragedy into triumph.

REASON 5: BEING THANKFUL STRENGTHENS OUR PRAYER LIFE

> I will confess, praise, and give thanks to You, for You have heard and answered me; and You have become my Salvation and Deliverer (Psalm 118:21 NASB).

Prayer is a remarkable privilege; one we often take for granted and fail to understand. There is the asking side of prayer, which includes seeking forgiveness, laying needs before God, and interceding for others. Then there is the appreciating side of prayer that includes praise, thanksgiving, and worship.

In dealing with sandpaper people, we need both sides. There will certainly be times when we must practice forgiveness and pray for that person who rubs us the wrong way. It is very difficult to stay angry with someone for whom we are praying. Prayer leads us to recognize and intercede for the needs in the life of each sandpaper person we know. At the same time, we can thank and praise God for working in that difficult relationship. Thankfulness strengthens our prayer life.

REASON 6: BEING THANKFUL SEALS THE VICTORY

> We will shout for joy when you are victorious and will lift up our banners in the name of our God (Psalm 20:5).

Victory and praise go hand in hand. Satan fully understands that when God's people live in an attitude of praise and thanksgiving, his schemes are doomed. By prayer, the power of God's Word, and thanksgiving, we declare our trust in God to deliver us. We lift up the shield of faith and make a frontal attack. Even in the midst of Satan's worst, we can find victory when we thank and praise God.

The last thing any sandpaper person expects to encounter is an attitude of thankfulness. Yet choosing to be thankful is a step God commands us to take. Right now, begin thanking God for allowing you to experience pain at the hand of a sandpaper person. Praise Him for the shattered dreams and crushed hopes that have come as the result of a difficult relationship. Trust Him to take what the enemy meant for bad and use it for good in your life. If you want to experience victory in your most difficult relationships, thank God for each and every one.

SANDPAPER T-SHIRTS

This is a great project for kids to do with adult supervision. A white cotton T-shirt, a few crayons, and a sheet of sandpaper are all it takes to get started!

Materials:

- Crayons
- Warming tray
- T-shirt
- Sandpaper

Steps:

1. Begin by placing a sheet of sandpaper (smooth side down) on the warming tray. The heated surface melts the crayon images as they're drawn, creating a painted effect.

2. Use the crayons to draw a design on the rough side of the sandpaper.

3. Insert a piece of cardboard or foam-core board between the front and back of the shirt, to create a flat work surface and protect the back of the shirt. Foil may be inserted directly under the fabric to enhance color penetration.

4. After allowing design to cool and dry on the sandpaper, place it face down on the T-shirt.

5. With a warm iron on the rayon setting, apply heat to the back (smooth side) of the sandpaper. Press the image for as much as ten seconds to re-melt the crayon design and transfer it to the fabric. Allow the shirt to cool.

6. To maintain the color, washing T-shirt on the gentle setting with cold water, then hanging it to dry is recommended.[14]

Be Committed:
Refuse to Walk Away

Let us run the race that is before us and never give up.
Hebrews 12:1 NCV

THE MAN WAS UTTERLY DISCOURAGED and disheartened by recent events. He had lost his job and was facing bankruptcy. His wife had left him, and his friends seemed to have disappeared. All that remained was his faith in God. While taking a walk, he stopped to watch some men building a stone church. One of them was chiseling a triangular piece of rock. "What are you going to do with that?" asked the discouraged observer. The workman said, "Do you see that little opening way up there near the steeple? I'm shaping this down here so it will fit up there."

Difficult relationships shape us down here to fit up there. The process is painful, but it's necessary to be more like Him. At times, it is so tempting to just give up, but getting along with people who rub us the wrong way takes a willingness to hang on and a firm

189

refusal to quit. Instead of sifting through solutions until we find one that is comfortable and fits our preconceived ideas of how to deal with difficult people, we need to seek God's voice in the matter, agreeing to follow His directions before ever hearing them. To say it another way, we must be committed, unwilling to walk away.

Commitment is always costly. Getting along with people who rub you the wrong way takes sacrifice, discipline, and a willingness to pay an enormous price. Because some sandpaper people are mates, family members, or children, it would be so much easier to file for divorce…walk away…or give up on the child who has broken every rule and your heart. Yet God uses each difficult relationship to refine and define us.

Commitment is the only right choice to make when dealing with a sandpaper person. We must be committed to staying in that relationship until God releases us from it. We must be committed to loving and accepting that abrasive person for as long as they are part of our world. But commitment is not just a grueling and tough standard that demands every ounce of strength we possess, it is far more—it is also the foundation on which God can build a life of worth, a life filled with meaningful and right relationships. Jesus defines and sets the standard for commitment in Matthew 22:37-39:

> "Love the Lord your God with all your heart, all your soul, and all your mind." This is the first and greatest commandment. A second is equally important; "love your neighbor as yourself." All the other commandments and all the demands of the prophets are based on these two commandments.

I recently saw a billboard that grabbed my attention—

> "That 'Love Thy Neighbor' thing—I meant it."
> —God

And He really does mean it, even when that neighbor is extremely hard to love. He only asks us to love our neighbor as ourselves *after* we have experienced His love and have completely surrendered to Him. We cannot love difficult people in our own power. It is a burden and a load we were never created to carry.

A few summers ago, our air conditioner wasn't working correctly. It only partially cooled the house, running night and day, doubling our already exorbitant electric bill. I called the repairman with a desperate plea for help. When he came to the house, the first thing he did was remove the filter from the vent. It was filthy, completely covered by some nasty gray gunk! Changing the air filter had never been one of my top priorities, as evidenced by the dirt and hair-caked object in front of me.

With a disapproving scowl wrinkling his weathered face, the repairman continued working, muttering under his breath. I pretended not to hear. He then removed the coil. Dangling it in front of my face, he pointed at the almost unrecognizable object and asked, "What is this?" My response was classic. "How am I supposed to know what that is? You're the repairman." In order to avoid his scathing glare, I closely examined it. It was covered with layers of dog hair, compliments of our West Highland terrier and Australian cattle dog; cat hair, compliments of Sassy, Chocolate, and Tiger; and dust, compliments of me! "Mrs. Southerland, this unit was never meant to work under this load. It's working as hard as it can, but it's not strong enough to do something it was never intended to do." The repairman then replaced the air filter, cleaned out the coil along with our bank account, and left the scene of the crime. However, the electric bill went back down, the house was cooler than it had been in months, and the unit worked like it was supposed to work. I forgave him.

> Sandpaper people behave in a manner that ultimately drives others away. Commitment looks past that behavior, sees the need, and chooses to stay.

God always honors commitment. Therefore, when we choose to love a sandpaper person, God honors that choice and fills our heart with His unconditional and always available love. Commitment is at the heart of God's love—but it's a rare commodity in our shallow quick-fix society. We want commitment to be easy and convenient, painless and cheap. However, commitment is none of those things.

In relationships, God calls us to the kind of commitment that never stops trying and never tries stopping. In Hebrews 12:1, we find a powerful picture of commitment: "We have around us many people whose lives tell us what faith means. So let us run the race that is before us and never give up" (NCV). Every part of the Christian life calls for commitment on our part, especially when it comes to the sandpaper people in our life.

James offers a deeper observation: "God blesses the people who patiently endure testing" (1:12 NLT). A commitment is a pledge or bond, a covenant or contract with no escape clauses or options for retreat. With people who rub us the wrong way, retreat often seems like the best option; interestingly enough, disappearance is actually the underlying goal of almost every sandpaper person I have ever known. While they desperately long for and need relationships, rather than risk failure, sandpaper people behave in a manner that ultimately drives others away. Commitment looks past that behavior, sees the need, and chooses to stay. Love that never gives up can hold on because of commitment, resolving to look past the circumstance while locking its gaze on the promise and covenant.

A Gift to Unwrap

Driving my daughter to school one morning, I heard a song I have come to love. The words describe the different people we meet every day and remind us that we might be actually encountering "the face of Christ." That unwanted intrusion in the form of a needy neighbor…that exasperating phone call from your least-favorite co-worker…an inept sales clerk who seems determined to work as slowly as possible…the grumpy old man who bags your groceries…an irritable and sick child who needs you every minute…may simply be God in your path. When dealing with an abrasive husband, an abusive parent, or a consuming child, realize that the face of that sandpaper person is really the face of God. It is amazing how He comes to us in so many ways. Look for "the face of Christ" and love Him wherever you find Him, even if it is in the life of a sandpaper person.

Sandpaper people are opportunities from God. How we respond to that opportunity and how we unwrap that relationship gift will determine the depth of the transformation in the life of that person and in our own lives as well. I know some sandpaper people will always be rough and coarse, refusing to change or even entertain the possibility of changing. In fact, they seem to enjoy rubbing people the wrong way. It is then that the love and grace of God is best illustrated. The fact is, God always uses the difficult relationships in life for the higher purpose of shaping us into His image.

Sandpaper people uncover the motives we try so hard to bury. The temptation is to look at the flawed life and the abrasive personality and discard the person, throwing them away like we would the daily garbage. What that mind-set must do to the heart of God! He is in the business of retrieving lives from the garbage dumps of sin and disgrace, cleaning them up through the forgiveness He purchased with His very blood, and transforming them into a priceless treasure that not only illustrates His power to change lives but testifies of His unwavering commitment to love the unlovable. When it comes to sandpaper people, we must do the same.

I love a great movie! To me, no matter what any movie critic says or how many stars the film is granted, a movie is only great when good wins over evil, the right guy gets the right girl, nobody gets hurt, and everyone lives happily ever after. A bit naïve, I know, but I have decided there is enough harsh reality traipsing through daily life without paying to see more on a movie screen. When I sit down in that cushy theater seat, popcorn and soda in hand, I want only happy endings.

With these criteria in mind, I went to see *Seabiscuit.* There I was, munching and sipping away, minding my own business and enjoying my brief respite, when a character's words soared off of the movie screen and slammed into my soul, yanking me back to the tenacity and unceasing power of truth: "You don't throw a whole life away just because it's a little banged up," he said. I was done! I thoroughly enjoyed the rest of the movie, but those simple words were written just for me and have lingered long after the credits scrolled down the screen.

The reality is, we are all "a little banged up." Sandpaper people are a little *more* banged up—in many ways and for many reasons. In *A Farewell to Arms* Ernest Hemingway writes, "The world breaks everyone and many are strong at the broken places." We all have both visible and hidden scars, fresh wounds and broken places. It is from pain that we can serve and learn to love those who are difficult...if we are willing to make the commitment to love the unlovable, accept the unacceptable, and learn from the ones we call sandpaper people.

Study and Application Guide

Chapter One
Be Loving: Recognize Their Worth

Key verse: "We are God's workmanship, created in Christ Jesus to do good works, which God prepared in advance for us to do" (Ephesians 2:10).

Key truths: Because we are the work of God, it is a spiritual discipline and step of obedience to see ourselves through God's eyes—as someone of worth and value. Sandpaper people often lack this perspective. Before we can love the difficult people in our lives, we must love God and ourselves.

APPLICATION STEP 1: BELIEVE GOD PLANNED ME

God planned and ordained each step before our first breath was taken and before our first cell was given life. We were planned and wanted in the heart and mind of God. So were the sandpaper people in our lives.

- Read Psalm 8:3-5. Evaluate the way you see yourself by the standards in this passage. What difference could this verse make in the life of a sandpaper person?

- Read Jeremiah 29:11. How does obedience to God's plan bring contentment? Explain this verse from the viewpoint of the woman at the well.

- Was her obedience to that plan a forced obedience or the natural result of her experience with God? In what way(s)? How does this principle apply to your life? The life of a sandpaper person?

- For the first time in her life, the woman at the well experienced contentment. Why? What message does her life hold for sandpaper people?

APPLICATION STEP 2: BELIEVE GOD VALUES ME

- The woman at the well couldn't see herself through the eyes of God. Why? Apply this truth to your sandpaper person.

- How can you explain this woman's lifestyle and sin in light of Psalm 139:13-16? Your own sin and lifestyle?

- In what way(s) can you identify with the woman at the well?

APPLICATION STEP 3: BELIEVE GOD PURSUES ME

- Read Isaiah 43:4. Insert the name of a difficult person in this verse and write it in your own words. Read it daily. At the end of the week, evaluate and pinpoint any changes you see as the result of this truth at work in your life. Record them in your journal.

- Read Romans 5:8. Was God's love for the woman at the well based on her repentance? Explain.

- Is our personal relationship with God based on our repentance? Explain.

- Memorize Romans 5:8. Make a list of the ways God has pursued you.

APPLICATION STEP 4: BELIEVE GOD CHOSE ME

- Read Jeremiah 1:5. Look back over your life. Identify the "special work" for which God has set you apart. How has He prepared you for that work?

- Identify the spiritual markers in your life. Record each one in your journal. List the approximate date, the experience, and the life change(s) that each marker made in your life. Copy the list and keep it in your Bible as a reminder of His presence and power at work in you.

- Read Ephesians 1:4. We all have a need to be chosen. How has this need impacted your life? How could it impact the life of a sandpaper person?

- What hedges of protection can we place in our lives in order to prevent a wrong self-image from taking root? Record them in your journal. Look for ways to reinforce these hedges.

APPLICATION STEP 5: BELIEVE GOD WILL CHANGE ME

- Read Psalm 40:1-3. Name the six changes God made in the psalmist's life.

- What one condition does the psalmist meet in order for God to make those changes?

- How has God changed your life? List the ways God has transformed your life. Praise Him for each one. List ways God could transform the life of your sandpaper person. Pray for each one.

My memory verse: "Before I made you in your mother's womb, I chose you. Before you were born, I set you apart for a special work" (Jeremiah 1:5 NCV).

Reflection points: Why do I resist change? What do I need to change in order to love my sandpaper person?

Chapter Two
Be Humble: Choose Against Pride

Key verse: "God opposes the proud but gives grace to the humble" (James 4:6).

Key truths: Newscaster Tom Brokaw tells the story of the day he was wandering through Bloomingdale's. He was feeling good about his well-deserved promotion to co-host of the *Today Show,* when he noticed a man watching him. The man kept staring, finally approaching him. "Tom Brokaw, right?" "Right!" said Brokaw. "You used to do the morning news on KMTV in Omaha, right?" Brokaw smiled. "That's right!" He waited for the praise to begin. "I knew it the minute I spotted you!" the man said. Then he paused and added, "Whatever happened to you?" Pride is a destructive element in any relationship with a sandpaper person. How can we choose humility over pride?

APPLICATION STEP 1: RECOGNIZE THE POWER OF GRACE

Sandpaper people long for and even demand mercy, desperately hoping they won't get what they deserve—justice. God offers grace. The life of the woman in Luke 7:36-50 was dramatically changed by God's grace. Read her story.

- Describe Simon in your own words. What was your reaction to his behavior? Is Simon a sandpaper person? Explain.

- Why would Jesus attend Simon's party? What does that say to you about the love of God?

• Why did the sinful woman come to the dinner?

• What was Simon's reaction to the presence of this woman? (When a rabbi was invited to someone's home, anyone could stop by and listen to the conversation.)

• Describe the significance of the woman's gift (see Luke 7:37).

Note: The small alabaster jar was common and of little value; it was the substance hidden inside that was precious. The perfume was the woman's most costly possession—very expensive, but very necessary in her line of work as a prostitute.

• Look up the word *abandon* in a dictionary. Record the definition in your journal. What part does "abandonment" play in humility? In dealing with sandpaper people?

APPLICATION STEP 2: TAKE CHARGE OF MY MIND

• Humility requires a disciplined thought life. Sandpaper people struggle with this truth. No doubt, the woman in Luke had to take captive every condemning thought in order to find Jesus. Read 2 Corinthians 10:5 and relate the importance of this truth in this woman's life.

- Read Luke 7:38. In regard to humility, what is the significance of the words "she stood behind him"?

- Why was this woman weeping in the presence of Jesus?

- Read Isaiah 26:3. What does it mean to "fix" our thoughts on Jesus Christ? Why is this important in dealing with sandpaper people?

APPLICATION STEP 3: KEEP THE BIG PICTURE IN MIND

Sandpaper people have tunnel vision. Life really *is* about *them*. In dealing with these difficult people, it's easy to inadvertently slide into their way of thinking; but in doing so, we lose sight of God's plan and purpose in our lives and theirs as well.

- What was Simon's real issue with the woman? With Jesus?

Simon lost sight of the big picture—the kingdom picture of God's forgiveness available to all. He'd become so focused on the "sandpaper" woman that he missed the redeeming work of God. Like Simon, we can become so focused on difficult relationships that we sacrifice kingdom thinking.

- Explain "kingdom thinking" in your own words. How does it apply to you?

- Read 1 Corinthians 12:7. Every believer has a gift that is meant to help the body of Christ grow and achieve balance. How can pride hinder us in using that God-given gift?

- In your journal, record the name of your most difficult person. Look for their spiritual gifts and list them next to their name. Pray for that sandpaper person to serve God with each gift.

- Read Luke 7:44-47. Compare the service of this woman to the service of Simon.

APPLICATION STEP 4: CHOOSE TO PRACTICE ACCOUNTABILITY

Sandpaper people have experienced very little accountability in life because they balk at the idea of submission. Submission is a God-ordained system of protection and accountability. God places people in our lives to see things we can't.

- List the people in your life to whom you submit. How has that submission brought good to your life? How has it affected your relationships?

- Look up the word *submission* in the dictionary. Record its meaning in your journal. Then record your personal definition of submission.

- Read Ephesians 5:21. What is the heart motive of submission?

- Luke 7:44-45 describes the humility of the sinful woman. List her acts of submission; then describe the result of that submission. How can you apply those same acts of submission to your relationships with sandpaper people?

APPLICATION STEP 5: UNDERSTAND THE REWARDS OF HUMILITY

- Read 1 Peter 5:6. What is our reward for choosing to humble ourselves before God?

- Read Luke 7:40-43. In your journal, write a brief summary of this parable. What was the reward for this woman's humility? What does that say to you about forgiveness?

Memory verse: "The Lord has told you what is good. He has told you what he wants from you: Do what is right to other people. Love being kind to others and live humbly, trusting your God" (Micah 6:8 NCV).

Reflection points: In your journal, record the main truth of humility God has shown you this week. Make a list of the ways you can "live" that humility as you deal with difficult people. At the end of the week, evaluate your life on the basis of humility and love. Record your evaluations and refer to them often as you seek to walk humbly before God.

Chapter Three
Be Accepting: Love Them—Just As They Are

Key verse: "Love one another just as I have loved you" (John 15:12 NASB).

Key truths: I love my children. While they sometimes make me angry, disobey me, and even disappoint me, when they are hurt or in trouble, the anger, disappointment, and even the disobedience are overruled by my love for them. If my imperfect heart responds to my children that way, think how God's heart responds to us when we hurt and disappoint Him. That is unconditional love and unmerited acceptance. How can we develop a love that never gives up?

APPLICATION STEP 1: CHOOSE TO BE FAITHFUL

A love that never gives up chooses to establish a faithful heart. It's the only hope for dealing successfully with the sandpaper people in our lives.

- Read Hebrews 13:8. How does this promise empower you to remain faithful in your relationships?

- Define *faith*. Compare your definition to the one given in Hebrews 11:1.

- Read 2 Chronicles 20:20. What is the reward of placing your faith in God? What does it mean to be "upheld"?

- Read Habakkuk 2:4. Describe the "crooked" life mentioned in this verse. Identify the "crooked" areas in your life and the life of your sandpaper person. List and commit each one to God's faithfulness.

- Using the word *faith*, create an acrostic that depicts the meaning of faith. Record it in your journal.

APPLICATION STEP 2: CHOOSE TO FORGIVE

One day, a man visited a church. He arrived early, parked his car, and got out just as another car pulled up beside him. The driver announced, "I always park there. You took my place." After moving his car, the visitor went inside, found an empty seat, and sat down, waiting for the service to begin. A woman approached him: "That's my seat. You took my place." Upset by the rude welcome, he said nothing and moved to another seat. When the service began with a prayer for Christ to dwell among them, the visitor stood, his appearance changing before their eyes. Scars appeared on his hands and sandaled feet, his eyes filled with love and compassion. The confused pastor asked, "What happened to you? Who are you?" to which the visitor replied, "I am the One who took your place."

Forgiveness is a frequent choice we must make and a habit we must cultivate when dealing with sandpaper people. As we choose to forgive, the Holy Spirit empowers that choice and supplies the forgiveness we need.

- Read Psalm 103:10-13. Write a paraphrase of this passage in your journal. Share it with a friend.

- Read Colossians 2:13-14. What does it mean to "cancel the record" of sin? How does this verse affect the way you deal with difficult people?

• List the sandpaper people in your life. Choose to forgive them, and across each name, write "forgiven." Each time you are confronted with those forgiven sins, speak the truth that you have already dealt with them, they are forgiven, and no longer hold any power in your life.

APPLICATION STEP 3: CHOOSE TO SACRIFICE

Sacrifice is the backbone of a love that refuses to give up and the underlying support of our dealings with sandpaper people. What sacrifices did God call Hosea to make? They are the same sacrifices God calls us to make.

• *Hosea sacrificed his* _____.

How important is your reputation? In your journal, list the good qualities others see in you. Are you willing to sacrifice the high opinion of others in order to love someone who has wronged you? Explain the ramifications of such a sacrifice.

• *Hosea sacrificed his* _____.

Think back to a time when a difficult person has mistreated you. Record the experience in your journal, including the way it made you feel. How did you handle your feelings? What actions did you take? Would you be willing to surrender the right to seek restitution?

Read Matthew 5:23. How does a refusal to forgive affect your service to God?

• *Hosea sacrificed* _____.

Read 1 Chronicles 21:24. What are the criteria for any offering we give to God? How important are your material possessions to you? Be honest.

The motive of the heart determines the acceptability of the gift. Read Acts 5:1-10. What consequences of greed are listed? Examine your own heart for any areas of greed. Record them in your journal. Ask God to forgive you and give you a heart willing to sacrifice.

APPLICATION STEP 4: CHOOSE RESTORATION

Most people I know find restoration painful and difficult to practice; but every relationship in life should include being accountable for the integrity of that relationship, no matter how difficult it may be. Restoration always demands an emotional and spiritual investment.

• Define *restoration* and record the definition in your journal. Is restoration an eternal investment? Explain.

• Read Jeremiah 15:19. What does God require from us in order to bring restoration? What is God's ultimate purpose in restoration?

• Read Genesis 3. Notice verse 9. God knew where Adam and Eve were, but He came in person, offering them the opportunity to repent. Just as He came looking for Adam and Eve, He comes to us. Eve may have been the first sinner, but she was also the first sinner to experience restoration from God. When has God restored you? Record the experience in your journal.

APPLICATION STEP 5: CHOOSE TO LOVE THE WAY GOD LOVES

God is a God of new beginnings and our only hope. Each time we experience the love of God through restoration and forgiveness, we gain new strength and wisdom to deal with sandpaper people. Love sees them through eyes of mercy.

• Define *mercy*. Write the definition in your journal.

• List several circumstances in your life when God's mercy has saved you from the destruction of sin. How should these circumstances affect your response to difficult people?

• Read Romans 8:38-39. Record these verses in your journal. Jot down any thoughts that come as you consider these words of Paul. What circumstances in Paul's life give credence to these verses?

Memory verse: "If you are standing before the altar in the Temple, offering a sacrifice to God, and you suddenly remember that someone has something against you, leave your sacrifice there beside the altar. Go and be reconciled to that person. Then come and offer your sacrifice to God" (Matthew 5:23 NLT).

Reflection points: What new commitment am I willing to make in order to love difficult people? Is there a relationship in my life in need of restoration? Am I willing to accept my sandpaper person—as is?

Chapter Four
Be Encouraging: Become Their Cheerleader

Key verse: "Do not let any unwholesome talk come out of your mouths, but only what is helpful for building others up according to their needs" (Ephesians 4:29).

Key truths: Sandpaper people are accustomed to being the target of harsh words. In fact, some difficult people delight in deliberately provoking strong words of criticism and condemnation in order to prove that what they really believe about themselves is true—they are broken and cannot be mended. God wants us to build up and encourage the sandpaper people in our lives.

APPLICATION STEP 1: UNDERSTAND THAT THE TONGUE IS A GIFT FROM GOD

- Read Psalm 35:28; Ephesians 5:19. Why did God give us the gift of communication?

- Mentally replay your conversations today. Examine your words in light of these standards. Using the acrostic below, write "yes" or "no" beside each question.

Were they **true**?	T	_____
Were they **helpful**?	H	_____
Were they **inspiring**?	I	_____
Were they **necessary**?	N	_____
Were they **kind**?	K	_____

In your journal, record these standards and employ them daily as a guard for your speech.

APPLICATION STEP 2: RECOGNIZE THE POWER OF THE TONGUE

• We underestimate the power of the spoken word. Read Proverbs 18:20-21. In your journal, write this verse in your own words. List specific examples from your life that substantiate the truths in this verse.

• Read James 3:2. What area of self-control does James mention first? Why?

• Read Hebrews 5:14. How does this verse apply to the control of the tongue?

APPLICATION STEP 3: USE WORDS FOR GOOD

One of the highest responsibilities in the body of Christ is to practice encouragement through our words. A word of encouragement may be a life preserver to someone drowning in a storm of life.

• Read Proverbs 10:21 and 1 Thessalonians 5:11. List the benefits of encouraging words.

• Read Proverbs 12:18. Paint a word picture depicting the damage reckless words cause.

- In your journal, record three memories of wounds inflicted by reckless words. Commit those memories to God's healing power. Write across each memory, "Healed."

- In your journal, record three memories of times when encouraging words kept you on your feet. Thank God for them.

- Write your personal commitment to control and use your tongue for good. Trust in God's power—not your own—to fulfill that commitment.

APPLICATION STEP 4: LEARN TO CONTROL THE TONGUE

- Do you agree with the statement, "We can promise to speak only good words but inevitably, that promise will be broken"? Support your opinion with Scripture.

- Read the verses listed below to discover the steps we can take to control our tongue. List those steps in your journal.

   —Matthew 12:34-35

   —Psalm 26:2 (In Darby's New Translation, "mind" in this verse is translated as "reins." Explain how this reminds us about the control of the mind.)

—Psalm 141: 3

—Ecclesiastes 5:2

Memory verse: "Set a guard over my mouth, O LORD; keep watch over the door of my lips" (Psalm 141:3).

Reflection points: Read Matthew 12:36-37. Contemplate the ramifications of its truth in your life. Record the verse and your thoughts in your journal.

Chapter Five
Be Patient: Learn to Endure

Key verse: "Forgetting what is behind and straining toward what is ahead, I press on toward the goal to win the prize for which God has called me heavenward in Christ Jesus" (Philippians 3:14).

Key truths: When I began working out with weights, I asked my son to help me get started. A rugged football player well-acquainted with the fundamentals of weight training, Jered graciously volunteered to be my personal trainer. While I expected soreness, I wasn't prepared for every muscle to scream out in painful protest! I wanted to quit—do what was easy, comfortable, and painless but still attain the toned body of a professional weight lifter.

Jered had no mercy and was committed to my success, encouraging me to keep working through the pain. One glorious day, he pointed out that those once painful muscles were no longer sore and seemed to be stronger as well. He even suggested it was time to increase the weight I was lifting because that beginning workout had become too easy! I was very comfortable with the beginning routine. That was the problem. Jered then said something I will never forget: "Mom, you get the greatest power from the greatest resistance." That's endurance.

The Holy Spirit has been given to us as a spiritual trainer, to lead us in the right spiritual exercises of life that make us stronger and more mature. Many of those exercises involve the submission of our will, the yielding over of our desires, and the choice to be patient with difficult people.

APPLICATION STEP 1: RECOGNIZE GOD AS THE SOURCE OF PATIENCE

- Read Romans 15:5. What is Paul's definition of patience? Why would Paul link patience and encouragement? How do they differ? Record your observations in your journal.

- Read Romans 15:4 and Deuteronomy 5:33. How does God give us patience?

APPLICATION STEP 2: CHOOSE TO BE PATIENT

Much of the Christian life is lived on the brink of right choices. Patience is no exception. We must continually make the choice to be patient—*before* we need patience.

- Read 2 Timothy 2:24. What does this verse say about the choice to be patient?

- Read Ephesians 4:22-24. In your journal, write a summary of these verses in your own words. What part does patience play in the truths voiced by Paul?

APPLICATION STEP 3: RECOGNIZE THE REWARDS OF PATIENCE

Threshing grain was a natural part of every day in ancient Rome. One man stirred up the sheaves while another rode over them in a crude cart on rollers instead of wheels. Sharp stones and rough bits of iron were attached to these rollers to separate the husks from the grain. This simple cart was called a *tribulum,* from which we get our word, *tribulation.* No Roman ever used his *tribulum* as a tool of destruction, only refinement!

• Read 2 Corinthians 6:4-10 in light of the above explanation.

• Compare the truths in 2 Corinthians 6:4-10 to dealing with sandpaper people. Record your observations in your journal.

• Read Romans 5:3-5. According to these verses, what should be our reaction to the presence and actions of the difficult people in our lives?

God uses our trials as tools of refinement and endurance builders. The word *endure* comes from two Greek words that, when combined, mean "to remain under." Endurance is the capacity to stay under the load, to remain in the circumstances without running away or looking for the easy way out. Sandpaper people train us to remain under the pressure of a tough relationship without running away or trying to escape.

• Define *endurance* in your own words. Record two circumstances where dealing with sandpaper people strengthened your endurance.

- Endurance is not passive. It is the picture of a soldier staying in the heat of the battle while pressing forward to victory! Read 1 Peter 4:12-13. Should we expect our faith to be tested? Why?

- Read Psalm 7:1. How can we expect God to work in and through our difficult relationships?

APPLICATION STEP 4: LIVE A PURE LIFE

- Read Ephesians 4:2-3. In your journal, list the qualities God expects us to employ when dealing with sandpaper people.

- What will be the result of our refusal to resolve conflict in a difficult relationship?

- Read Psalm 51:10-12. Why is this scripture a formula for patience?

- A clean heart produces a "steadfast spirit." Steadfast means "fixed or unchanging." Compare a steadfast heart to the heart of a sandpaper person. In your journal, describe the part a steadfast heart plays in dealing with sandpaper people.

APPLICATION STEP 5: LIVE AN OBEDIENT LIFE

While vacationing in the mountains, a man watched a lumberman working beside a mountain stream. He would occasionally jab his sharp hook into a log, separating it from the others floating downstream. When asked about his selections, the lumberman explained, "These logs may look alike, but a few of them are very different. The ones I let pass are from trees that grew in a valley. They were always protected from the storms, and their grain is coarse. The ones I hook and set apart came from high up on the mountains. From the time they were small, the trees were beaten by strong winds, toughening them and giving them a beautiful grain. They're too valuable to use for plain lumber. We save them for our best work."

- Compare the patience and strength you gain from dealing with the difficult people in your life to the truths in the above illustration. Record the comparison in your journal.

- Read 2 Corinthians 6:7. In this verse, "truth" literally means "integrity, or deeply rooted righteousness." How does applying God's truth affect our daily lives?

- Look *righteousness* up in the dictionary. Record its meaning in your journal and add your own definition.

- Read James 1:2-3. What should be our response to trouble? How does testing affect our faith? What characteristic does a tested faith produce in our lives?

Memory verse: "Be still before the LORD and wait patiently for him" (Psalm 37:17).

Reflection points: Read Isaiah 40:29. How does this promise apply to patience? To endurance? Throughout the week, think about how God gives you the strength and power you need for dealing with people who rub you the wrong way. Praise Him for that work.

Chapter Six
Be Forgiving: Forgive and Forget

Key verse: "If we confess our sins, he will forgive our sins, because we can trust God to do what is right. He will cleanse us from all the wrongs we have done" (1 John 1:9 NCV).

Key truths: I've always hated wearing shoes. As a child, I looked forward to summer—summer days found me outside playing, shoes and socks left behind. The first few days were rough on my feet; pain and bruises were meted out by the merciless gravel road on which we played. It only took a couple of weeks for the transformation to occur, though. What were once tender, soft feet became callused, tough feet that could run down that gravel road without hurting at all, the pain of the early summer days forgotten.

Sin is the same. The first time we commit a sin, it really hurts. Continued sin hardens the heart and builds spiritual calluses in the soul. The day we are comfortable in our sin is the day we take up residence in enemy territory, inviting failure into our lives. God is serious about sin. We need to be as well.

APPLICATION STEP 1: CONFESS SIN CONTINUALLY

- To *confess* means to agree with. It is a present-tense verb, meaning we must confess sin continually, without stopping. What benefits do you see in dealing with sin this way?

- In your journal, record a time when you allowed sin to harden your heart. How did it affect your everyday life? Your relationships? Your fellowship with God? What broke through that hardness, bringing you back to the place of repentance and surrender?

- What does "confess" mean to you? Record your answer in your journal.

APPLICATION STEP 2: CONFESS SIN COMPLETELY

Honesty and transparency *before* God always leads to forgiveness and restoration *from* God. Jesus paid the only price sin requires. Confessing sin creates an awareness of and sensitivity to sin that eventually becomes a deterrent from sin.

- Make a "sin sheet" in your journal. Ask God to reveal every sin in your heart. Record each one on your "sin sheet." Allow time for the Holy Spirit to work. You don't need to worry that He will miss some sin lurking in the darkness in order to "hold that sin over your head" later. That is neither the heart nor character of God, but rather is a frequent cheap shot of Satan. Even more than you want to be clean before God, He wants you to be clean before Him. Thank God for revealing your sins. Confess each one. If the sin is between you and God alone, mark it off of your list. If the sin involves someone else, restitution may be necessary. Make things right with them; then mark the sin off of your list. When you have worked through the entire list, take a red permanent marker and write "1 John 1:9" across the sheet of paper. Thank God for His perfect plan of forgiveness.

- Read and memorize Psalm 103:12. When the enemy accuses you of confessed sin, speak this verse aloud, knowing that God has already forgiven and removed this sin from your life.

APPLICATION STEP 3: CONFESS SIN CONFIDENTLY

- Read Psalm 38:18. What does the confession of sin accomplish?

Once we confess sin, we can put it behind us. God is just and fair, seeking only one payment for sin. Jesus made that payment—nothing else is needed. One of Satan's favorite tactics is to bring up past sin, accusing us while dumping a load of guilt on us. We can and we must stand against him, not trusting our feelings but the facts of God's word. And those facts are clear—when we confess sin, God forgives and removes that sin from our spiritual account, bringing the balance of condemnation to zero.

- In what areas of your life does condemnation exist? What sin is feeding that condemnation? Come to God in confidence, knowing He will forgive and forget your sin.

APPLICATION STEP 4: IDENTIFY AND ELIMINATE THE ROADBLOCKS TO FORGIVENESS

- Identify the roadblocks to forgiveness present in your life. Ask God to help you remove each one.

- Read Mark 11:25. How does refusing to confess sin hinder our spiritual growth?

APPLICATION STEP 5: RECOGNIZE AND CHOOSE TO TAKE THE STEPS OF FORGIVENESS

Knowing we need to give and receive forgiveness is not enough. We must *take action*. In the blanks below, record the steps of forgiveness listed in chapter 6.

1. Take the _____.

2. Forgive _____.

3. Forgive _____.

4. Practice _____.

5. Pursue _____.

- Read Proverbs 28:13. What are the consequences of trying to hide sin? What are the benefits of confessing sin?

- Which step is the hardest one for you to take? The easiest? Why?

Memory verse: "Be kind to one another, tenderhearted, forgiving one another, even as God in Christ forgave you" (Ephesians 4:32 NKJV).

Reflection points: Read John 19. In your journal, record your thoughts and reactions while reading John's account of Jesus' death on the cross.

Chapter Seven
Be Caring: Meet a Need

Key verse: "The greatest among you must be a servant" (Matthew 23:11 NLT).

Key truths: In a ghetto lived a little boy who believed in God. That belief made him the frequent target of other children in the neighborhood.

They taunted him, "If God loves you, why doesn't He take care of you? Why doesn't God tell someone to bring you shoes or a warm coat? Where is the food you've been asking God for?" With tears streaming down his dirt-stained cheeks, the little boy said, "I guess He does tell somebody but somebody forgets." The spiritual investments we make are eternal investments. The compassion of God at work is such an investment—it's called *service.*

Service is not an option for the Christian. It is a joyful command! The most contented people I know are the ones who serve the most. Your mission field is your home, your office, your neighborhood, and every sandpaper person who resides in your world. If you want to be contented, look for opportunities to give yourself away in acts of compassion and care.

APPLICATION STEP 1: SEE THE NEED

- Read 1 John 4:8. In your journal, write this verse in your own words. Record your definition of love.

- What does it mean to love like God loves? Explain the truth that if we do not love, then we do not know God.

- Read 1 John 4:20. Can we love God without loving others? Can we love others without loving God? What relationships in your life display the unconditional love of God?

APPLICATION STEP 2: FEEL THEIR PAIN

Sandpaper people are in great pain, but they have failed to deal with or work through that pain. Empathy is a gift we bring to the table when dealing with people who rub us the wrong way.

• Read Galatians 6:2. Part of spiritual obedience is sharing the pain of others. What specific actions does a commitment to feel the pain of others require? How does that commitment affect you on a daily basis?

• Think back to a crisis in your life when someone shared your pain. Record that experience in your journal. Write a note of thanks to the person(s) who helped and comforted you during that difficult time. Then write a note of compassion to your sandpaper person.

APPLICATION STEP 3: TAKE IMMEDIATE ACTION

• Read 1 John 3:17-18. In your journal, write these verses in your own words, as if you were speaking to someone in need.

• Think back over the last month of your life. Has anyone met a specific need? If so, what was your response?

• Identify one need in the life of your sandpaper person. Set a time limit. Make a specific plan for meeting their need in a specific way. Record that plan in your journal.

APPLICATION STEP 4: MAKE A LONG-TERM PLAN

• Read Galatians 5:13. We are to serve each other with _____ .

- Read 1 Peter 5:2. What is the heart attitude of a true servant of God? Examine your heart to see if that is your attitude as well. If not, what is standing in the way? Identify and eliminate that roadblock.

- Describe the role of a shepherd. Read Psalm 23 every day this week, asking God to make you sensitive to the needs of others and empowering you to serve His sheep. At the end of each day, record new insights gained from this passage.

APPLICATION STEP 5: ALWAYS FOLLOW UP

- Read Colossians 3:12. What kind of "clothes" are you wearing today? In your journal, list the five qualities mentioned in this verse. Describe how each quality is important to a follow-up plan. How can these qualities equip you for dealing with the difficult people in your life?

- Read Matthew 20:28. Define "servant." Record the definition in your journal. List three ways you have been a servant this week.

- List five people you can serve. Assign each person to one of the next five weeks. Make a plan to serve each person—in one way—each week. Record each experience in your journal. Be sure to include the changes these acts of service bring to your life.

Memory verse: "I am the vine, and you are the branches. If any remain in me and I remain in them, they produce much fruit. But without me they can do nothing" (John 15:5 ncv).

Reflection points: Think about the sandpaper person with whom you struggle most. Have you ever considered that person to be a "mission field"? Contemplate a new commitment today, a commitment to make eternal investments in the mission field of your relationships.

Chapter Eight
Be Peaceful: Wage Peace

Key verse: "The peace of God, which surpasses all understanding, will guard your hearts and minds through Christ Jesus" (Philippians 4:7 nkjv).

Key truths: We sometimes assign the responsibility for our peace and happiness to people or things. Our needs can only be met in God. Sandpaper people are notorious for seeking peace from their circumstances and from the people with whom they interact. Frustration and anger is the result.

There is a "God-shaped hole" in each one of us. We frantically search for things to fill that void, only to discover that none of them can. The emptiness remains, and a seed of anger is planted. The heart of a sandpaper person is weary from that search, tired of turmoil, and in desperate need of God's peace.

When we surrender to God, He immediately fills that "God-shaped hole" with His presence. It's a perfect fit! Peace takes up residence as we learn to wholly lean on Him, but relationships with no peace are doomed to fail—especially difficult relationships. In the key verse, Paul states that the peace of God will guard our hearts and minds. The guard is Jesus Christ. His presence ushers in an unexplainable calm that grows from a heart contract between child and Father. That calm becomes our tutor in dealing with anger.

- Read Colossians 3:8. In your journal, describe the progression of sin that begins with anger. What conclusions about the power of anger can you draw from this verse?

- Think back to a circumstance in your life where anger was destructive. In your journal, record that experience. What lessons did you learn from that circumstance? How have those lessons impacted your life? What hedges of protection have you put in place in order to guard against the destructive power of anger? List them in your journal.

- Using a concordance, look up other verses pertaining to "anger" and record them on 3″ x 5″ index cards. Carry them with you and commit the verses to memory.

Every relationship occasionally requires a response to anger-filled words, attitudes, or actions. In relationships with sandpaper people, sparks fly easily, igniting a relationship war and battle of wills. We always have a choice, when it seems there is no choice, in how we respond.

- Read 1 Timothy 2:8. Is it possible to worship God while harboring unresolved anger?

- What conditions for true worship are listed in this verse?

APPLICATION STEP 3: ADMIT YOUR ANGER

• Nehemiah admitted, "I am very angry!" What keeps you from admitting your anger?

• Think about Nehemiah's position. Put yourself in his place. In your journal, record the thoughts and emotions you think he experienced in choosing to openly admit his anger. Would such an admission affect his reputation? How?

APPLICATION STEP 4: DISMISS YOUR ANGER

• Read James 1:19-20. Fill in the blanks below using these verses. In your journal, use these three admonitions to create a formula for dismissing anger.

    Be quick to _____.

    Be slow to _____.

    Be slow to _____.

• Have you ever mistakenly acted on your anger instead of simply dismissing it? What were the results?

APPLICATION STEP 5: RESOLVE YOUR ANGER

• Read Ephesians 4:26. Is it possible to be angry and still not sin?

- What is God's timetable for resolving anger? Explain the benefits of quickly resolving anger. Describe the consequences of harboring anger.

- List two ways you have learned to resolve and control anger:

  1. _____

  2. _____

- List two ways you can prevent anger from taking root in your life. List scriptures from this chapter to support your ideas:

  1. _____

     Scripture:_____

  2. _____

     Scripture:_____

Memory verse: "Those who do not control themselves are like a city whose walls are broken down" (Proverbs 25:28 NCV).

Reflection points: What masks has anger worn in my life? How has anger hurt me, and how has my anger hurt others? What are some hedges of protection I can place in my life to guard against anger?

Chapter Nine
Be Confrontational: Care Enough to Confront

Key verse: "Faithful are the wounds of a friend" (Proverbs 27:6 NASB).

Key truths: When Jered and Danna were small, Dan and I alternated taking them to the pediatrician for baby shots because we both hated going! Taking a healthy, happy baby to the doctor only to emerge later with a screaming child in need of Tylenol made no sense—until the doctor explained, "Mary, I know it's hard to watch your babies being given shots when they are perfectly healthy." So far, he was right on the money. "Think of it this way. A little pain now prevents a bigger pain later." What a perfect picture of confrontation!

The art of confrontation is a gift from God to every relationship in our lives—especially those difficult relationships. Confrontation has the potential to turn a sandpaper person into a velvet person and a difficult relationship into one of great joy.

APPLICATION STEP 1: CONFRONT WITH THE RIGHT MOTIVE

- Read Matthew 7:2-6. Compare "sawdust" with "plank." In your journal, describe the requirement Matthew explains.

- Define *hypocrite*. Record the definition in your journal.

- Describe a relationship in which you were the one with a speck of sawdust. Then describe a relationship in which you were the one with the plank. Compare the two.

- What did Matthew mean when he said we would "see clearly" how to confront?

APPLICATION STEP 2: CONFRONT IN THE RIGHT WAY

- Gentleness is not weakness. It is controlled strength. Apply this truth to the art of confrontation. Why is *gentle* confrontation so important?

- Using this chapter, fill in the blanks below to list the seven elements of confrontation done the right way:

  1. Always begin confrontation with _____.

  2. Be willing to _____.

  3. Express hurt—not _____.

  4. Make clear and _____ statements.

  5. Avoid using the words _____ and _____.

  6. Learn to _____.

  7. Be _____.

- Which one of these elements do you need to work on first? Why?

• Read 1 Peter 3:8. List the five qualities of someone who is prepared for confrontation.

APPLICATION STEP 3: CONFRONT AT THE RIGHT TIME

• Explain the relevance of the following statement in the confrontation process: "The only difference between a foul ball and a home run is timing."

• Describe the ramifications of confronting at the wrong time versus the right time.

• Read Philippians 4:14. Explain the importance of the word "when" in this verse.

APPLICATION STEP 4: CONFRONT WITH THE RIGHT AUDIENCE

• The disciplined person can do *what* needs to be done *when* it needs to be done and *where* it needs to be done. Read Proverbs 23:12. Explain the importance of discipline in this step of the confrontation process.

• How would it make you feel if someone confronted you in public? Record your thoughts in your journal.

APPLICATION STEP 5: CONFRONT WITH COMMITMENT

Read Romans 12:18. Some people refuse any kind of helpful confrontation and have no desire for peace. In fact, they feed on volatile eruptions and explosive relationships, relishing the pain they inflict and, sadly, the pain they experience. Their hurt has become an identity they are unwilling to relinquish. Even so, we still have a spiritual responsibility to that person and to God.

- Describe a time when confrontation didn't work as you expected. What was your reaction?

- Fill in the blanks below:

  1. Go back and _____ on that person.

  2. Accompany that check with an act of _____.

  3. _____ for that person.

  4. Give them a little _____ and _____.

Memory verse: "Think of ways to encourage one another to outbursts of love and good deeds" (Hebrews 10:24 NLT).

Reflection points: What is your greatest fear about confrontation? What are your greatest strengths and weaknesses in confrontation? Did Jesus confront anyone? Make the commitment to resolve any conflict in any relationship and be willing to confront if necessary.

Chapter Ten
Be Strong: Develop Endurance

Key verse: "He gives strength to those who are tired and more power to those who are weak" (Isaiah 40:29 NCV).

Key truths: Strength and endurance are fed by discipline. We sometimes consider discipline to be a negative character trait. Not so. Discipline is simply a wholehearted "yes" to God.

My husband and I pulled up in front of our brand-new townhouse, excited over the events of the evening. Dan was a youth pastor at the time, and we were returning from a Monday-night Bible study where several high-school youth had accepted Christ. We were flying high—until we saw the shattered glass and opened the front door to chaos and the debris of an invasion. We had few "valuables," but several items that had been stolen were priceless because of their personal value. My mother's nursing watch, Dan's guitar and leather strap, a gift from his first youth group, and our sense of security—all stolen. I felt vulnerable and insecure.

A lack of discipline allows the same thing to happen in our spiritual life. "A person without self-control is as defenseless as a city with broken-down walls" (Proverbs 25:28 NLT). Strength is lost in an undisciplined life, while endurance grows in a life wholly committed to godly discipline.

APPLICATION STEP 1: CHOOSE DISCIPLINE

• Read Proverbs 3:11-12. What should be our response to the discipline of God? Why?

• Do you agree with this statement, "God is committed to our character, not our comfort"? Explain.

• Define discipline in your own words and record your definition in your journal.

• What changes do you believe discipline will make in your life?

APPLICATION STEP 2: CHOOSE HUMILITY

- Read 1 Peter 5:6. What does God promise He will do when we humble ourselves before Him?

- Define humility and record the definition in your journal. List the characteristics of a humble person. How many of these characteristics are present in your life?

- What part does humility play in discipline?

APPLICATION STEP 3: CHOOSE PEACE

- Read 1 Peter 5:8-9. How does this verse apply to discipline?

- Read Psalm 94:12. List the rewards of discipline in your journal.

- What roadblocks to peace are present in your life? In your relationships?

- What steps do you need to take in order to remove those roadblocks?

APPLICATION STEP 4: CHOOSE WISDOM

- Fill in the blanks below from Revelation 3:19.

    "Those whom I love I rebuke and discipline.

    _____ and _____."

- Compare your attitude toward discipline to the attitude described in Revelation 3:19. What changes do you need to make in order to choose the discipline of wisdom?

APPLICATION STEP 5: CHOOSE FAITH

- Read 1 Peter 5:10. What do you think "make everything right" means in your life?

- What rewards of suffering are mentioned in this verse?

- Use a concordance to locate "faith" verses. List five of them below. Memorize one of them this week.

    Faith verse 1 _____

    Faith verse 2 _____

    Faith verse 3 _____

    Faith verse 4 _____

    Faith verse 5 _____

Faith memory verse: _____

_____

_____

Reflection points: Would you describe yourself as a strong person? What is the source of your strength? Is it enough?

Chapter Eleven
Be Thankful: Thank God for Them

Key verse: "When you ask [God], be sure that you really expect him to answer, for a doubtful mind is as unsettled as a wave of the sea that is driven and tossed by the wind" (James 1:6-8 NLT).

Key truths: Dealing with sandpaper people requires faith. We often say we need more faith, when in reality we operate in faith every day. We flip a switch, believing light will appear, or turn a key, believing the car will start. We see an unfamiliar doctor, who writes a prescription we can't read. We surrender it to a pharmacist we've never seen, who gives us a medicine we cannot pronounce, and we take it—all in faith. Instead of asking for more faith, we need to exercise the faith we already have.

APPLICATION STEP 1: HAVE FAITH

Difficult relationships are cluttered with unrealistic expectations. When dealing with sandpaper people, we often rely on our own tactics and solutions instead of walking in faith.

- Read 1 Thessalonians 5:18. How does this verse apply to your sandpaper person?

- What strategies have you used in dealing with your sandpaper person? Were they successful?

- What step of faith do you need to take in your relationships with difficult people?

APPLICATION STEP 2: THANK GOD

- Do you really believe that thankfulness helps us measure our problems against His limitless power, turning stumbling blocks into stepping-stones? Explain.

- Read Psalm 43:4. What does it mean to "go to the altar" in dealing with difficult people?

- Why does faith bring God pleasure?

APPLICATION STEP 3: GIVE SACRIFICIALLY

- In dealing with sandpaper people, we must learn to make a variety of sacrifices. List five sacrifices you have had to make in a difficult relationship. List the attitude with which you made the sacrifice.

Sacrifice	Attitude
1. _____	_____
2. _____	_____
3. _____	_____
4. _____	_____
5. _____	_____

- Read Psalm 50:23. Define "thank offerings" and explain the part they play in dealing with sandpaper people.

APPLICATION STEP 4: CHOOSE VICTORY

God always desires to transform tragedy into triumph. In dealing with difficult people, this concept is especially compelling.

- Read 1 Peter 1:7. Fill in the following blank using this verse. A genuine faith is always_____. Explain your answer.

- Write one paragraph describing the refining work of God through your most recent difficult relationship.

APPLICATION STEP 5: CHOOSE PRAISE

Fill in the blanks below using the chapter as a guide.

- Being thankful _____ our spirit.

  Being thankful strengthens our _____ _____.

  Being thankful devastates _____.

- Read Psalm 68:4. Paint a word picture of this verse in your journal, explaining its significance in regards to sandpaper people.

- Read Psalm 118:21. According to this verse, why can we praise God?

- List the sandpaper people in your life. Beside each name, write a sentence of praise. Pray those praises each day. Record the difference these praises make in your attitude toward sandpaper people.

Memory verse: "We will shout for joy when you are victorious and will lift up our banners in the name of our God" (Psalm 20:5).

Reflection points: How has my lack of faith hindered improvement in the difficult relationships in my life? What part does faith play in dealing with difficult people? What faith commitment am I willing to make?

Chapter Twelve
Be Committed: Refuse to Walk Away

Key verse: " 'Love the Lord your God with all your heart, all your soul, and all your mind.' This is the first and greatest commandment. A second is equally important; 'Love your neighbor as yourself' " (Matthew 22:37-38).

Key truths: We are to love God with all of our heart, which means to love Him completely from the center of our being. We are to love Him with all of our soul, which is our very essence. Finally, we are to love Him with our whole mind, the place our identity is forged and then worked out in our lives. God calls us to total commitment to Him. It is from that commitment we are empowered to love our "neighbor."

APPLICATION STEP 1: BE COMMITTED IN LOVE

- Read Matthew 22:37-39. Defend the statement that commitment is a product of love.

- What part does commitment play in true love? Can love be authentic without commitment?

- Why is this kind of commitment necessary to deal with sandpaper people? What part does commitment have to play in difficult relationships?

- Read Romans 8:37 and explain why victory is the fruit of God's love.

APPLICATION STEP 2: LET GO AND LET GOD

- Why is commitment so crucial to your relationship with God? How does God bless the committed life?

- What commitments has God made to you concerning the sandpaper people in your life? If you are not aware of any, ask God to show you each one. Record them as He brings them to mind.

- What commitments have you made to God concerning sandpaper people?

- Read Romans 8:31 and apply this truth to commitment. Record your thoughts in your journal.

APPLICATION STEP 3: BE FREE IN CHRIST

- Read Galatians 5:1. Discuss the correlation between freedom and commitment. How do these truths apply to your relationship with sandpaper people?

- Read 1 Peter 1:13. What two directives does Peter give concerning self-control? What rewards of self-control are mentioned in this verse?

APPLICATION STEP 4: MAKE COMMITMENT A LIFESTYLE

- Read Philippians 2:5. What changes in your lifestyle have to be made in order for your thoughts, attitudes, and behavior to line up with God's standards?

- Examine your life for those areas needing commitment to God. Spend time in prayer releasing each area to Him. Make a list of the changes you need to make. Record your thoughts in your journal.

- Do you think it is wrong to love yourself? Explain.

APPLICATION STEP 5: NEVER GIVE UP

- Read Hebrews 12:1. Write this verse as if you were speaking to your sandpaper person.

- Read James 1:12. What quality does God produce in us through testing? How is that quality important in dealing with difficult people?

Memory verse: " 'Love the Lord your God with all your heart, all your soul, and all your mind.' This is the first and greatest commandment" (Matthew 22:37).

Reflection points: Write down five new thoughts on commitment. Using the word *commit,* create an acrostic that will be a reminder of the commitment God made to us and the commitment He calls us to make to others.

Final Thoughts

When you complete these Bible studies, I encourage you to read back over your journal to evaluate your growth in learning to deal with sandpaper people. Celebrate how far you have come.

Reflect on the healing and restoration God has accomplished through the study of His Word.

Rejoice in all God will do in your relationships because of your obedience to these new truths.

Now is not the time to stop and rest in new knowledge.

Now is the time for obedience.

God will honor that obedience by bringing His peace, purpose, and power to every relationship in your life.

Personal
Journal

JOURNALING CAN BE A VITAL TOOL in spiritual growth. Recording new truths, insights, and promises from God cements His work in our lives. As you work through the Bible studies, the Holy Spirit will "nudge" you in the right direction and whisper fresh, eternal realities to your heart and soul. The enemy would like nothing better than for you to ignore those nudges and discard the realities. I encourage you to write them down! Read them repeatedly. As you remember the victories and celebrate the hand of God at work in your life, His presence will become a powerful reality. One day, your journal will become a testimony to and record of God's faithfulness for those who come behind you.

_____

_____

_____

_____

_____

_____

_____

_____

_____

_____

_____

_____

_____

_____

_____

_____

_____

_____

_____

_____

_____

_____

_____

_____

_____

_____

_____

_____

Notes

1. "Sandpaper 101," www.woodzone.com.
2. "Sandpaper Numbers," www.montessoriworld.org.
3. C.S. Lewis, *The Four Loves* (New York: Harcourt, 1960), p. 121.
4. "Sandpaper Dreams," www.hyperdictionary.com.
5. "Bush Tucker Plants," www.teachers.ash.org.au.
6. "Fletcher's Frog," Wildlife of Sydney Fact File, www.facnanet.gov.au.
7. "Music Blocks," www.music.vt.edu.
8. Idea Box, www.theideabox.com.
9. "Sandpaper 101."
10. "Sandpaper 101."
11. "Sandpaper 101."
12. Adapted from "How to True Your Tires," www.slotcarillustrated .com.
13. "Sandpaper 101."
14. Adapted from "Sandpaper Transfer T-Shirts," www.diynetwork .com.

Coming Out of the Dark:
A Journey Out of Depression
Mary Southerland

As a pastor's wife and mother of two adorable children, Mary Southerland had a life filled with wonderful things . . . until clinical depression brought her world crashing down. Mary found herself in a horrible pit, but she also slowly discovered the way out. And now she offers biblical insight and practical steps to freedom with the refreshing transparency of someone who has been there and intimately knows the pain of what you and your family are experiencing.

As one of America's fastest growing health problems, depression touches one in three people. If you struggle with depression, have a loved one dealing with depression, or simply need encouragement during a bleak time of life, *Coming out of the Dark* will help. It will guide you to the One who is light and who will be right beside you to comfort and encourage you from the beginning of your journey to its end—a place of wholeness, joy, and freedom.

When You Need a Miracle:
Experiencing the Power of
the God of the Impossible
Lloyd John Ogilvie

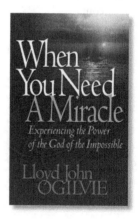

Are your greatest needs—with family, work, relationships—going unmet? Are you limiting your life to only what is possible in your own strength and talents? From his longtime pastoral experience, Dr. Ogilvie points the way to the God who can meet your *every* need because He is Lord of the *im*possible— the One who can bring about miracles of healing, reconciliation, and growth!